Regrets

A Flatlanders Story

THE KID

Copyright © 2024 **Daryl Shaffer Publishing**
All rights reserved. No part of this publication may be reproduced, distributed, or transmitted in any form or by any means, including photocopying, recording, or other electronic or mechanical methods, without the prior written permission of the publisher, except in the case of brief quotations embodied in critical reviews and certain other noncommercial uses permitted by copyright law. For permission requests, write to the publisher, addressed "Attention: Book Rights and Permission," at the address below.

Published in the United States of America

ISBN 978-1-962730-31-0 (SC)
ISBN 978-1-963379-83-9 (HC)
ISBN 978-1-963379-84-6 (Ebook)

Daryl Shaffer Publishing
222 West 6th Street
Suite 400, San Pedro, CA, 90731
darylshafferpublishing.com

Ordering Information and Rights Permission:

Quantity sales. Special discounts might be available on quantity purchases by corporations, associations, and others. For details, contact the publisher at the address above.

For Book Rights Adaptation and other Rights Permission. Call us at toll-free 1-888-945-8513 or send us an email at admin@stellarliterary.com.

Dedicated to Mom and Pops

For Their

Sixty Eighth Wedding Anniversary

About The Author

   The Kid grew up in the Midwest, a Flatlander. Followed his dreams of adventure to Montana. Where he got the chance to live out his dream of being a Montana Cowboy. Where he still lives today after 46 years.

Contents

Acknowledgments vi
Introduction viii
Arrived at the Ranch 1
The Kid's First Day 5
Old Brown 33
Breakfast and Town 45
Fixing Fence 64
The Kid's First Branding 88
Cattle Drive 99
Cow Camp 107
Hairpin 125
Tracks 166
Change Is A-Coming 187
Good-Byes 203

Acknowledgments

A small group of wonderful people helped me to live out a young boy's dream. Those people who started as strangers turned into friends who will forever fill my heart and mind with wonderful memories of fun and adventure. I would like to take the time now to give thanks publicly to all those friends who are living and the few who have passed. They were such a cast of characters who, by chance, became a large part of this wonderful period of my life.

Therefore, I have, with pleasure, written their names in this book to give them recognition of how important and memorable their friendships have been to me over the years. Without their participation, I would not have had the opportunities they took the time to make known to me. I would have just missed all the chances to have the adventures if it were not for their nudging and eventually pushing.

I have also given recognition to other friends—animals—which somehow never get the credit they deserve. These animals gave their unconditional affection and friendship to me, if only for the short time we spent together. That is also why I am giving their names recognition in this book—as an additional thank you. I do it with the hope that it will somehow ease my memories of their passing as well.

A friend of mine once said that when you die, you go to a special place where all those friends who have touched your heart are waiting for you: heaven! What an absolutely wonderful belief, and with all of my heart, I hope this is true. I miss all these friends so very much!

The time I have spent remembering was most wonderful and nostalgic. Over the years, I have tried enthusiastically telling my stories to many of my friends in the west, merely to have all my storytelling efforts falling on deaf ears with looks of "Here he goes again!" They never quite know whether the stories are true or if maybe the Kid is just stretching the truth again. So let me say this to them and to you, my new audience.

Over the years, I have heard other people tell their own stories with the same excitement—famous people. Although I am not nor do I want to be famous in my life, I feel this was for me similar to catching the touchdown pass to win the Super Bowl, making a putt on the eighteenth green to win the Masters, or maybe, just maybe, even walking on the moon!

Last, my hope in writing this book is to encourage all my readers to chase after their dreams. It does not matter what your beginnings are, you can still dream and you can still live the life that is out there for you to discover! It is never too late to look up at the stars and say "What if," to say, "This is what I want to do with my life," taking the chance! You never know, you could end up having the time of your life!

Now I am looking forward to my good friends back home and you reading about a young man who moved from the Midwest. Through luck, he lived out his childhood dream of working on a Montana ranch as a cowboy!

After growing up in the Midwest, I never really imagined having the adventures that one could only read about in books or watch in movies. Now that I am in the fall of my life and looking back, I have had just the best life so far. What a ride! I am not saying the good times are over, but maybe it's time to reflect awhile, take a breath, a nap or two, and think about what I want to do next. But for now this is a Flatlanders story to tell!

Introduction

Once upon a time, there was a young boy who could lose himself reading western books and watching cowboy movies. The timeline was the early 1960s. It was a time when you could turn the Kids loose after school and for the summer without the worries a parent has today. Children could just roam around, play, and invent things to do!

When this young boy was growing up, it was surviving a day at a time. His father had died when he was ten, leaving his mother to raise four boys by herself. Since this young boy did not have much time with his father and his mother worked providing for her boys, he looked for guidance.

The young boy looked to his best friends' parents, Mom and Pops, in combination with books, movies, and sports to get the mentoring he needed to become adult. These resources became a large part of who he is today.

When he was growing up, actors like John Wayne and Clint Eastwood, and books like those written by Louis L'Amour, especially the Sacketts series, were a huge influence. There was always some western hero who came out of what seemed to be nowhere to lend a hand. They dressed so cool, in cowboy hats, chaps, silk bandanas, and boots, with spurs jingling. They used that western lingo, like, "Howdy, ma'am," with a tip of the hat; they were and are so cool! Watching and reading about those western heroes helped him fight the fight of good versus evil!

As the boy got older, it was hard not to get caught up in the everyday struggles of life. He had a job, car payments, and insurance; he started to set aside his dreams. People who were happy in their own lives surrounded him.

The young man felt that he was the only one who wanted something more! It was so hard for him to break that connection with his beginnings.

After graduating from high school, his best friend, Dick, wanted to visit relatives in Montana. They loaded up his friend's Oldsmobile and drove the two thousand miles west.

As they drove away from their home state of Ohio, he could not believe the changes. The country was changing—the badlands, Yellowstone National Park, and eventually the Rocky Mountains! It was right out of the books and movies he had read and watched!

Just as you drive into Montana, there is a national park at the place where the Indians fought Custer, winning the battle against Yellow Hair. The young man saw signs all over telling him to watch out for rattlesnakes. Cool!

Eastern Montana is prairie with lots of sagebrush and open country. It is still beautiful. As they drove from Livingston toward Bozeman, he saw the Rockies for the first time. Wow! He just could not believe anything could be so outrageous, so beautiful. Even then he knew this was where he wanted to be—the Rockies!

They drove on to Missoula, hitching up with his best friend's relatives. They were great. They took them to Flathead Lake and then to Glacier National Park. Now you have to be kidding! Up to that point in his life, there had been nothing like Glacier National Park. Even now, it is hard to believe there is anything on earth so beautiful. He had never been anywhere like it, then or now!

They stayed with his friend's relatives for part of the summer, and the vacation was great—all of it. He could not remember any time or place in his life that made such an impression. That trip gave the tangible evidence that the books and movies were real. There was a place where there were cowboys, Indians, and snow-capped mountains; it was Montana! He thought this would be the place for him to find adventure.

Once he arrived back home, he could not think of anything else. But he had to be patient, because Montana was not in his original plan. He had to do some thinking and make a different plan, one that would get him back to Montana.

The young man was almost twenty-two years old when he arrived back in Montana to live. Dick, his best friend, had already moved to Montana and been working for about six months. It was great to renew the friendship and get started on his new life.

After he had spent a few months living in Montana, his best friend decided to move back home to Ohio. He had given it his best shot, but he missed his family and friends. This was a great disappointment. They had known each other since the seventh grade, and his parents were his adopted family. But the young man was still very determined to stay, because he had just gotten to Montana!

The young man found a job with the forest service working with individuals his age, eighteen to twenty-three years old, in YACC (Young Adult Conservation Corps). YACC was a government program that gave work training in the timber industry.

The job was great for him. It covered room and board and paid him some money. He was able to save a little money spending time in the woods as a recreational supervisor in the after-work activities. His supervisor (Nan) was a blonde swimmer from Arlington, Virginia. They hit it off from the start. Can you imagine? His life just got a whole lot better. Go figure!

They had a lot in common. They both played different sports, and they both were athletic. She was a swimmer from Arlington, Virginia; he played golf and a little football.

At the time, he weighed about 285 pounds and was six feet six inches tall. He had packed his free weights so that he could continue working out to stay in shape. They both worked out. He lifted his weights, and she swam an unbelievable number of laps in the lap pool. Boy did he ever get tired of counting her laps! Nevertheless, it was great hitching up with someone who understood a commitment to a healthy lifestyle.

After about year and a half, Nan gave him a want ad out of the newspaper for ranch hand for hire. She thought since that is what he often talked about, watched in movies, or read about in western books; he should go do it because his time working with the YACC would be over once he turned twenty-four. He set the ad on his dresser and went about his life.

The young man still cannot remember for sure how long the ad sat there. Maybe a couple of months? But one day he decided to call the phone number from the newspaper.

To this day, he does not know why he had not thrown the little piece of paper away. Why was the job still available? He could not tell you. He called the number and agreed to the job. After hanging up the phone, the young man thought he had gone and done it now. The job started the beginning of the next month!

The young man had the right amount time to give notice and say his good-byes. He was taking a chance on the unknown and leaving his friends again. His good-bye to Nan was especially hard. The young man didn't have a clue as to what he was getting himself involved in, not to mention leaving her! It just had to be the stupidest thing to do. The young man really thought he would have a chance to work on a ranch for the summer, have some fun, and hitch back up with Nan when all this adolescent connection to cowboys and Indians was over.

So he said his good-byes and started on his trip to the ranch.

Arrived at the Ranch

When leaving Missoula and going into southwest Montana, a person from the city really has no feel for how big the country is. A young man could get lost, never seeing civilization again.

After driving for a few miles in southwest Montana, the country started to change. He saw sagebrush, it was drier and open, and there were barbed wire fences, jackleg fences, and miles and miles of fences. There were cattle everywhere and horses. He really expected to see the Duke, Hoss Cartwright, or Rowdy Yates trailing a bunch of cows!

The ranch ended up being on the Montana–Idaho border in the Rocky Mountains. After the phone conversation, he had learned that the ranch had been in the family from the first homesteaders. The two-story main house was a pretty good size of about 2,500 square feet. The very rustic-looking log house was built the second time after the Indians burned down the first log house. You have to be kidding!

The rest of the ranch buildings were as the owner said, very old and very western, just like you would imagine. The horse barn was or seemed to be the original structure of logs. The cookhouse was newer, made from rough-cut lumber from a sawmill. But the bunkhouse was made out of logs—yep, the bunkhouse!

When driving into the ranch, it looked deserted. The owner said he would see him when he got here. There was really no specific time. As he walked around checking things out, he had no idea of what to think except he had arrived for what was to be the start of his summer on the ranch!

After a while, June showed up after picking up groceries in town. She looked to be in her late fifties and was very cordial. They sat for a while trying to get to know each other. She said that her husband, Paul, would be in for dinner directly. He was out feeding the cows. The young man just smiled with anticipation at seeing a real cowboy!

Soon there was some commotion at the mudroom door, and then Paul, with his dogs, came in. He looked to be in his late fifties, around six feet with a slender build, and a big gray-and-black beard with chewing tobacco juice running down it. The old cowboy wore jeans and a Levi jacket, chaps, a cowboy hat, a red silk bandana, and cowboy boots with spurs making the noise spurs make. If any of the young man's cowboy heroes from books or movies would have walked through that door, they could not have looked any different. Wow! The real cowboy's dogs were blue heelers, Sam and Helper. Helper's name came about this way: Sam had got together with a female heeler, and she had pups. Out of that litter, Paul picked out a female pup to help Sam with his work, Sam's helper, Helper. What a great way to name a dog!

The larger-than-life cowboy walked in, talked briefly with the cook, and then walked back out without any introduction. After the real cowboy walked out of the cookhouse, the young man smiled, looking back at the cook. He must have had a look of "are you kidding?" surprise on his face. The cook just smiled, saying he should go help Paul load the wagon with hay. The young man from the Midwest could not get out the door quick enough!

At the haystack, there was a tractor hooked up to a wagon with loose baler twine wrapped around the front uprights. The real cowboy was there lifting bales, with the young man helping load the small two-string wild grass bales, which weighed about fifty-five to sixty-five pounds each. The moment in time had the young man from Ohio excited, to say the least. The wagon was loaded in no time. Paul smiled at him saying, his first words: "Kid, you will do."

When the real cowboy and the Kid arrived back at the cookhouse, June looked surprised. "Done already?"

Paul just smiled and said, "The Kid likes bucking bales." June smiled, telling the Kid to go wash up and have some dinner.

At dinner, there was homemade everything: chicken noodle soup with big, thick noodles, pie, cake, and sourdough bread fresh out of the oven. You get the picture! The Kid was in food heaven, and boy could he eat! June watched, and Paul just smiled, saying, "Looks like the Kid likes to eat too!"

It was not to long after dinner had started that the owner showed. They introduced the Kid to the owner, now the boss. After the Kid had devoured all his food, the boss walked the young man to the bunkhouse, with the Kid taking the room at the end of the log building.

The room was small, with an old leather couch, a small double bed, and yes, a very old wood-burning pot-bellied stove for heat! The outside of his room had gaps between the logs and would need chinking between most of the logs. He really didn't believe anybody had used the room in many years.

The boss told him to take the rest of the day to move in and to be at breakfast at 6:30 a.m. Work started at 7:00 a.m. He said, "Fine, but one question. Where is the bathroom? Where is the running water?" The boss pointed to a small room at back of the cookhouse, about thirty to forty yards away. The young man from Ohio really did not know what to think and nodded saying, "That will be fine." It did take him the rest of the day to clean out his room and move in. Up to that point, the Kid really had not acquired that many belongings. He had some clothes, none of which was what you would wear to work on a ranch.

But the young man from Ohio did have two very important possessions at that time: his golf clubs and free weights. He thought there had to be a golf course close by, and there was definitely time for him to work out with his weights to stay in shape. That's why he chose this room—to work out, of course. He had to stay in shape and not let his conditioning go to waste. Besides, he was only going to do this for the summer. He would have some fun and get back to civilization after the summer was over.

He ate supper, another homemade meal of lasagna and homemade sourdough bread with sweet cream butter for the spreading. The Kid was in his little room thinking this was going to be where he lived for the next few months, and already it felt a little like home with the fire burning in the pot-bellied stove.

Paul and June seem to be real nice folks, and the boss seemed nice as well. But he smiled, and he still could not believe what might be on the horizon waiting for him the next morning. Breakfast was at 6:30, and He had to get to bed for a good night's sleep.

"Paul, what do you think of the Kid?"

"Seems willing enough to work. He tossed around those bales like there was no weight to them at all! The Kid is as big as a bear. I don't think there is a horse around that the Kid could ride! Has the Kid said how long he plans to stay and work?"

"Paul, it hasn't come up. At least he can help with the chores and help you do the rest of the feeding. If the Kid would work just through the summer, it would be a great help! It wasn't too long ago you were in the hospital with a stroke!"

"Yes, old girl, I am doing fine. As long as you keep the grub coming, I will keep doing fine! But did you see the Kid eat? We are better off feeding him in the barn!"

"Let the Kid eat all he wants. You know he is not going to get it in his wages. Might as well eat as much as he can. Besides, I like it when the hired men eat what I put on the table."

"Well, old girl, I do not think you are going to have a problem with that one. Let's hope he is finished growing! I'll get him up in the morning and see if I can get him to help me milk old Buttercup. That will tell me a lot if she will behave herself; then we have someone to at least milk that old milk cow!"

"Paul, do you think the Kid has worked around stock before? Buttercup can be awfully cantankerous to milk!"

"I will find out tomorrow morning. As far as I know, the Kid is from the Midwest, a flatlander. Now we will have all the answers soon enough. Let's get some shut-eye."

The Kid's First Day

While the Kid sat staring at all the new clothes he had bought from the mall's big and tall store, the screen door to the cookhouse opened and slammed shut. He looked at his watch. It was close to 5:00 a.m. He thought someone else was having a hard time sleeping.

There were footsteps coming in the direction of the bunkhouse and then a banging on his door.

"Hey, Flatlander, get some clothes on. Come help with the milking! Have to pay for all that grub you ate last night and earn your keep! I'll be in the barn getting old Buttercup ready for you."

The Kid just stared at the door. He had never milked a cow. What was the cow's name, Butter Who? And who the heck is "Flatlander"? Besides, work was not supposed to start until after breakfast, at 7:00 a.m.! The Kid quickly finished putting on some of his new clothes and ran out the door. Walker, trailing the milk cow into the barn, smiled as he saw the Kid run down to the barn in his tennis shoes and golf cap. The dogs ran right up to the Kid, playfully biting at the bottoms of his new pant cuffs.

"Kid, this is Buttercup, your milk cow."

"I have a milk cow?"

Walker led Buttercup to the head catch in the milking pen, putting grain in the feed tub for the old milk cow. Next the old cowboy started to give the flatlander his first chore on his first day working on the ranch—his dream!

"Kid, the old milk cow can be a little ornery at times! Sometimes it helps to massage her back and sides before you sit down to begin milking the old swing bag. Best to use this soft horse brush.

"Now Kid, get down like this and sit on the stool. You have to clean all of the dirt from her teats and bag like this. Put the milk bucket in this position between your feet. Put a little bag balm on your hands like this. The salve will keep you from making her teats sore. You place the top of your head in this position, and you grab a teat in each one of your hands like this. You alternate with your hands until those two are empty and start on the other two. Now let's see you give it a try."

The Kid sat on the stool, placed the bucket between his feet, and started to milk Buttercup.

"Now before you go any further, you want to place your head here at the flank. That will give you the best chance to know if old Buttercup is about to kick! By placing your head here, you can feel her hip move. It might someday keep you from being kicked. Now hurry, we have to get finished before she gets done eating her grain, so we have to work fast!"

At first, it was slow going, and old Buttercup didn't know if she liked the Kid. She even tried to turn her head in the head catch to see who it was. Paul and his dogs were watching the Kid milk, and then it happened, bang! Buttercup took a kick, missing the Kid, but tipped over the milk bucket in the process.

"Wow, Paul, that was quick. That old cow can move pretty fast!"

"Yes, she can. Now place the top of your head in the flank. You will be able to feel the kick coming. There you go. You seem to have the knack of it now. I am going to catch my horse. You keep on milking that sweet old Buttercup. I'll be just a few minutes.

The Kid listened to the old cowboy's footsteps going clear to the other end of the barn and began milking Buttercup with a new sense of urgency. The milk was slowly going into the bucket in little squirts when the old cow arched her back, bunched up her hips, and started to relieve herself!

"Oh my God, Paul, the old cow is going to the bathroom. You have to be kidding!" Laughing, the Kid saved the milk bucket, backed away from the old cow, and waited for her to finish. When she was done, he just stood leaning against the barn wall smiling in disbelief.

He waited for what seemed to be an appropriate time and then cautiously resumed milking.

Walker was finishing saddling his horse when the Kid came walking down the barn, grinning with the milk bucket.

"Well it looks like you had a good time milking your first cow. Let's see if you got a full bucket. Well, not too bad. You will get more this evening before supper. She generally gives a bucket full at each milking before breakfast and before supper. What did you do with the old cow, and who were you talking to?"

"I didn't do anything with her yet, and I was trying to get your attention! When you didn't answer, I figured I would get myself and the bucket of milk to a safe place first! Does your dear sweet Buttercup always relieve herself when you're trying to milk her? I was lucky to get out of the way!"

"Well, she is your milk cow now, and it is kind of hit and miss on bowel movements! But no harm, you did get dear, sweet Buttercup milked, and I saddled my horse. But we had better turn the old milk cow out. Have you ever operated a tractor?"

"No I haven't, but I will lay money down that it won't kick or try to relieve itself on me," he said, smiling.

"That is good. A sense of humor goes a long way out here on the ranch! But let's go by the tractor so we can warm it up while we're eating breakfast."

"Well, by looking at the milk bucket, the old cow must have been a little ornery!" said the cook.

"She wasn't too bad. She just tried to kick and pee on the flatlander, but he has a sense of humor about it!"

"Paul, it is always good when a person has a sense of humor around you! Lord knows, I have needed mine for a long time cooking your meals!"

"Now, old girl, you know you love me and my dogs to pieces!"

"Yeah, I love you, and especially those dogs of yours. Who could live without those two heeling troublemakers! It was not enough having Sam. You had to have a female out of the dog. She has been trouble from the start. Heck, Paul, no one has been able to sit in that chair since you got her! She just lays underneath that chair hoping some fool will sit in it!"

The Kid had sat there last night before supper, and she didn't seem to mind.

Walking through the mudroom door, the Kid heavily sat where he had the night before, in Helper's chair. After watching the huge stranger block out any possible light from the sun, feeling her world was coming to end, Helper nipped at his heals just like the night before!

The cook frowned at the old cowboy. "Kid, you better get up to the table and get some breakfast!"

The Kid was hungry. He felt like he had already put in a day of work or at least a start to one. He had a huge stack of homemade sourdough pancakes with warm chokecherry syrup, big, thick slices of crisp, honey-cured bacon, fresh over-easy eggs, and a glass of fresh milk to wash it down.

"Hey, Flatlander, where on God's green earth did you learn to eat like that?"

"Well, Paul, I think it comes sort of natural to me. It surely helps that this is the best grub I've eaten for a long time. Wow!"

"You better slow down; June is going to have more on the table for dinner!"

"Paul, let the Kid alone. I like to watch him eat. He reminds me of a pack of hungry wolves!"

They sat eating their food, having a conversation about what was supposed to happen the rest of the day. Walker asked if the Kid had run any equipment before, tractors and such. He said no. Walker asked the Kid if he had any experience working with stock. He said no, just dogs and cats. Walker asked if the Kid had any experience building or fixing fence or digging postholes. He said no. Walker asked if the Kid had any experience living in the mountains and dealing with the weather that is characteristic of the higher elevation. He said no. Walker then asked his last question.

"You are from the Midwest, a flatlander. You have no apparent background in ranching or what you might get the chance to call mountain weather. My question is this: you are really not that old, but why is it that you want to start doing it now?"

"I have always read books and watched movies about the West. It just seems like it would be a great way to live! Being from the Flatlands, as you call it, the Midwest is nothing like the mountains. Besides, already I have eaten some of the best grub of my entire life! If not for my lightning-quick reflexes, dear old Buttercup would have kicked me and then relieved herself all over this flatlander. I feel I have just started what surely has to be one heck of a good time. So if you're done with the questions, I see a few strips of bacon that should not go to waste."

With breakfast over, it was time to get on with the morning work. Walker, the dogs, and the Kid walked out to where the tractor was warming up, and the old cowboy gave the Kid a quick course in how to operate a tractor.

The tractor is a relatively new compared to the rest of the place, a 2510 series John Deere with a front loader. Walker showed him all the basics: clutch, gears, hydraulics, and most of all that it was a diesel tractor that used diesel fuel, not gas!

"Now do you have any questions?"

"Seems like it's straightforward."

Walker, riding his horse and followed by his dogs, led the Kid the quarter mile to the first gate. The Kid took just a minute to look at the scene. There was an old cowboy and his dogs leading the way for him, the flatlander from Ohio, on a ranch in the middle of the Rockies! It was certainly a similar to a scene he had read about or even watched in movies. But to be doing it was a little hard to believe. He was going to have a great summer!

The distance gave the Kid the time to tinker with the tractor, messing with the hydraulic controls for the front-end loader; up and down the bucket went. The bucket also had a top set of forks in order to grab hay. He had to open and close that many times. The only operation the Kid seemed to have a problem with was the clutch. He had only operated automatic transmissions up to that point in his life.

Since they were a little behind schedule, the yearlings were all bunched up at the jack gate waiting to be fed. Walker stopped his horse, and without any prompting, his dogs cleared the area around the gate of yearlings. It was the first time the Kid had the chance to see real cow dog's work! The dogs were grabbing at the yearlings' heels. First one and then another, yearlings were sent in turmoil of kicking and bucking, a stampede, the Kid thought!

Walker waited until the dogs finished, and from his horse, he unlatched the gate, swinging it open. The Kid popped the clutch, lifting the front end of the tractor off the ground. Walker just smiled, motioning for the Kid to continue.

"Kid, just stay in the seat. Don't let her buck you off!"

Smiling, the Kid noticed there was what looked to be more than a few hundred yearlings in a pretty good-size pasture covered in cow pies—lots of cow pies! As the Kid drove the tractor, he scanned the field for anything interesting. There was a creek that ran through the field with willows on each side. On the far side of the creek, there was a bench of land covered with sagebrush.

After riding his horse to an open area of the field, the old cowboy motioned the Kid to stop. He sat on the tractor watching as Walker tied the stud to the back of the hay wagon. Then from there, the old cowboy walked toward the tractor, with the dogs clearing a path through the yearlings that were full of curiosity and mischief.

Almost on the brink of laughing, the Kid did not know really what to do or think. The excitement and energy that the cows exhibited was fun to watch. They butted each other with their heads and had pushing contests with their faces flush against one another, looked almost like they were playing football. There was kicking, bucking, and most of all, maneuvering to get closest to the wagon. But when any yearling tried to get close to Walker, his dogs would send them in a rush of running and bucking.

While smiling, the old cowboy said, "Well, we made it this far, Flatlander, and I see you stayed in the saddle. Good for you!

"Here is how it's going to work. I want you to put the tractor in low range, low idle with the steering going straight. Then come get on the wagon with me. Sam and Helper will clear out any yearlings that get in the way of the tractor."

"Paul, do we always let the tractor run in the field by itself?"

"Kid, the tractor is in low range, and with the Sam and Helper keeping the yearlings from getting run over, it will be fine. It is important to know that when feeding hay, you feed it out a little at a time. You don't want to feed hay in big clumps. Whether it be yearlings, cows, or bulls, it is best to feed hay out in a steady stream. The animals eat more, and the weight gain on the animal is better. So, when you cut the string, just let the bale leafs dribble off the wagon." Walker and the Kid fed the rack of hay from both sides while the dogs cleared the way.

The next gate was a double jackleg pole gate just like the one they had just gone through. Walker made a point to tell the Kid that this gate had to be closed at all times. The big field they were about to go in was empty for now, but it was empty to keep the yearlings out of the cows, which, by the way, were the yearling's mothers last calving season. They used the field as a buffer between the two. There were no shortcuts in leaving this or any gate open to make things easier. The rule of thumb is how you find the gate is how you leave the gate, no exceptions!

The field they were entering was a lot rougher. There were deep washouts and a couple of culverts for crossings that he needed to show to the Kid. There was only one way to get from one gate to the other. If you missed it, you could find yourself in a whole bunch of trouble, and time would be lost. Walker asked him to take note and remember this information for when he was by himself trying to cross the field.

Weaving the next few miles over culverts and ditch crossings to the next gate, like the yearlings, the cows were at the gate waiting for the cowboy to feed them. But there was something different; there were calves everywhere!

Walker rode his horse up to the gate, waiting for the dogs to clear away the cow and calf pairs. This time the cows were a lot more subdued, allowing the rider, dogs, and hay wagon into the field. The whole scene was a lot more manageable, the Kid thought.

As they got further into the field, there were groups of calves hanging out with one or two cows. The young calves were fun to watch. They played the same games as the yearlings but not quite as rough. They were running, jumping, and kicking with the same excitement but always keeping their mom in sight or at least another calf's mom. The groups of cows and little calves reminded the Kid what it looked like in nurseries.

"Paul, I have never been around calves before. How old are they?"

"Those are this year's calves. Some started calving in early February and some want to take their good old time and have yet to get the job done."

Staying at the stack yard, the Kid watched as the old cowboy fed the loose hay with the tractor. Beside him were Sam and Helper crouching, with heads low to the ground, staring at any cow that might have the idea of coming into the stack yard. Helper considered the flatlander in that description and could not resist in grabbing at the Kid's pant cuffs.

"Now you are going to get me in trouble with Paul. You had better stop what you are doing!"

"Kid, quit playing with my dog!"

Glaring at both kids, Helper's dad seemed to take it upon himself to get in between the two troublemakers.

Helper's dad, Sam, like all dads, was an altogether different kind of cat or dog, as he may be. He looked like he had been in a lot of fights and was partial to having a serious attitude about anything that crossed his path in a bad way.

Sam wasn't an altogether tough-looking blue heeler. However, for being two years old, he had plenty of scars to show the women in his life. The flatlander even thought his coat, with a black and gray saddle with speckles of the same colors, made him look a little on the tough side, but he was nothing to write home about. But it was his stare; Sam's eyes would look at you, and you had better figure out what he had on his mind, because trouble was fast coming your way!

"Listen, Kid, Sam and Helper are my dogs. They're not to be played with—and by the way, Sam will bite if aggravated! So maybe this is a good time to fill you in on my working stock. Plain and simple, all of my animals, heck even the cook—well, she can probably take care of herself—are an investment of a lot of time and energy to have got them to this point. I do not want you or anybody else trying to change their mind of who is the boss! Now you are new and need some time to get acquainted with how things are done here on the ranch, but that is about the way the working animals are handled on the ranch, or at least mine are."

Walker went back in the stack yard, grabbing another bunch of hay, with Helper following the tractor, looking in the Kid's direction. When Helper left, Dad moved to the middle of the opening to the stack yard, giving the Kid a look as if to say, "This is my job, find something else to do!"

Walker went out into the field a little distance and started to drop his load slowly, little by little until the loader was empty. It was obvious what Walker was doing and Helper did her job, so none of the pairs got in the way of the process.

"OK, Kid, do you have any questions?"

"Yes, how much do I feed?"

"Just enough hay that when you come back in the morning, there is just a little left, but that will change due to a few different things. First, the weather conditions. The worse the conditions, the more the cows will eat and waste. A pregnant cow or a cow that has a calf is eating for two. They will eat more. The size of the animal, cows versus yearlings versus bulls, that matters as well. It all gets down to feel, and you only get that after you have done some feeding for yourself. Let's get you started. I will be watching you as I check the cows for any trouble. The dogs need to stay here while I check the cows in the willows. Sam will stay with you, and Helper will be at the stack.

The Kid started feeding, and Walker rode over to the willows to see if he could find any cows calving. Sam and Helper did as Walker asked them to do, although the Kid didn't see any verbal instruction from him. The dogs just seemed to be able to check the situation out and do what they needed to do. The partnership between Walker and his dogs was remarkable, as if the dogs were just another pair of hired hands that had been working together long enough that it left little to talk about.

That is how it went. The Kid was on the tractor feeding hay to the pairs, and Walker was checking for cows calving. The Kid was enjoying being by himself, even if Walker was reasonably close by. It gave him time to concentrate on things he was learning without someone being right there looking over his shoulder. Working with people always made the Kid nervous, and Walker was no exception, especially since he had walked right out of the pages of a Western novel.

After the Kid fed for a while, he liked the relationship that feeding the animals gave him. How it made him feel working around them was a surprise. It had only been a few hours, but he felt a real sense of doing something good. There just seemed to be a nice pace to everything so far.

It was not to long until he had fed enough. There were just a couple more buckets. All the cows had their heads down eating, with some of the older calves mocking their mothers, and the calves that were in groups were playing as if they did not have care in the world. It was cool to watch!

Walker was now coming over from the willows, riding his horse so easily. There did not seem to be any effort on his part or the horse's part.

"Looks like you are getting used to the tractor. Just a little more should be good. I am going to take the dogs and check the cows on the bench across the creek. When you get back home, load the wagon with hay for tomorrow, the same amount as we did yesterday. That should make it in time for dinner." Walker rode off with his dogs to check on more cows, with the Kid going back to feeding the last of the hay.

Watching Walker and his dogs ride off into the mid-morning daylight, the Kid thought to himself, *Guess there is no hand holding! That's fine by me. Now let's get the wagon hooked up and start making our way back to the ranch.*

The old cowboy rode through the cows very slowly, checking for any sign that one might be ready to calf. Walker could ride through the cows as if he were looking in on a friend who was sick, just there for support. He could maybe see if there was anything he could do to make things a little easier while the friend was under the weather.

Also, we should note that Walker was old school. There were no fancy calving sheds or newfangled apparatuses. He liked to give the cow a chance to calf alone with as little help as possible, the way old Mother Nature intended!

As Walker rode through the pairs, there are many different signs he looked for. The cow's bag would start to swell with milk a couple weeks before it was time for her to calf. When she was really close, the teats would fill with milk, starting to drip a little if it was time. The cow's body language was another good way of checking for signs. He would look at how she walked and if there was a little arch in her back, a little waddle. She would start to maneuver herself away from the other cows to be by herself to start the process. He would see if she was lying down and not chewing her cud, maybe feeling a little uncomfortable. The sign he could see from a distance was about half the tail would stiffen, sticking up toward the heavens about at a forty-five-degree angle. This meant her water bag probably was hanging out her back side or even broken. She had started to calf.

The cows he was riding through had been around him since they were young. He knew which ones had an easy time of it and the ones that had trouble. He knew to a large degree where a cow was going to calf. The old cowboy seemed to recognize each of them as if they were old friends. This was all done by the different physical characteristics of each cow—the color, facial features, length of tail. There were similar differences in cows just like people. You just had to take the time to look hard enough; they were there.

Walker went through the door of the mudroom, with his dogs going to their blankets by his big leather recliner. By this time, the Kid was walking through the outside door behind the old cowboy.

"Paul, how did calving go?"

"There is one old cow that is getting ready. Little feller could be sucking her momma before I am able to get back. How did it go for you?"

"Just fine. There were a couple yearlings that tried to give me a little trouble! But I was able to get the gates shut."

"Well how did the morning go?" the cook asked.

"I guess, old girl, we did well all around. The Kid here was able to get through the morning without too much trouble. The cows are doing well, and I believe there will be a new calf on the ground when I get back. Maybe the flatlander will get to see a brand-new calf. But for now, I hope you have something the Kid can eat. Looks like he's a little hungry!"

"Well let's see, we have leftover homemade chicken noodle soup with the big, thick noodles that you like so well. Additionally, we have fresh sourdough bread just out of the oven. Now for dipping in the creamy chicken broth, you probably need to put a little sweet cream butter on the bread before you dip. Now if that does not fill you two up, there are fresh-baked cinnamon-glazed apples for dessert!

That was all it took. The Kid slid his feet, and Helper nipped both his heels.

"Kid, you really got to be smarter than my dog. But now that you're standing, set yourself up to the table and see if you like leftovers."

June and Paul just watched as the Kid devoured his food. He didn't even seem to take a breath. He looked like he had not eaten for days!

"Take it easy there, Flatlander. The cook made plenty for everyone!

The conversation then turned to what they needed to do after dinner. The Kid had to go back to the yearlings to feed bags of protein pellets with the old Dodge flatbed. Walker tossed him the keys. The old cowboy would go with the Kid and show him where to load the bags and how many. After that, they had to feed the bulls some hay in the bull pasture that borders the cookhouse. Then before supper, old Buttercup needed milking.

By the time the dinner conversation was over, the Kid had eaten two big bowls of homemade chicken noodle soup and half a loaf of fresh-baked sourdough bread, butter, and honey for dipping in the soup. After he had eaten the baked apple, he used his fingers to get the rest of the cinnamon glaze out of the bowl. Then he was full!

"Hey, June, if the Kid keeps this up, you won't have to wash his dishes! Maybe I should take the Kid with me to cow camp. Between him and the dogs, I won't have to clean any dishes!"

The Kid just leaned back in his chair, needing to take a breath. "June, that is as good as it gets! That was the best soup. Heck, all of it was the best I have eaten since I moved out west!"

"Hold on there, Flatlander, the cook is mine. I will not give her up for nobody!"

"Kid, what in the world have you been eating, and more to the point, who has been cooking it?"

"June, I have really never taken the time to learn since I moved west. I just have eaten whatever has been handy."

After enjoying his dinner, the Midwest flatlander kid waddled over to the old Dodge flatbed with keys in hand. The old Dodge looked like it had seen its better days. It had bald tires, a cracked windshield, and side mirrors that had long since been involuntarily removed. "Oh, there is no driver's door handle." So, reaching through the space where the window should have been, he grabbed the inside door handle and opened the driver's door.

The interior smelled of mice, that musty smell. There were springs for seats. Someone had put a couple pillows on the seat for padding, and here it comes, a stick shift!

The Kid opened the door to the pickup and sat on the driver's seat pillows. While sitting all pillowed up, he was surprised to see an am/fm radio with an eight-track player. Cool! He thought maybe he still had his *Rocky* theme on tape. He loved that music from the *Rocky* movie, "Gonna fly now!" He thought maybe he would like to have it now, because he had never driven a stick shift!

Then, shaking his head, singing a little music, he thought, *what the heck? It can't be any different than operating the tractor.*

So the Rocky wannabe looked at the knob for the shifting pattern. Thinking he had found neutral, he turned the key, and it started! He pushed in the clutch, shifting to what he thought was first. Letting out the clutch, the truck died. He tried it again, and it died again. He tried again, and it died again!

Walker had been watching over at the bags of pellets. He had seen enough and walked over to lend a hand.

"Kid, how we doing?"

"Not so good. I should have said something, but I had never driven a stick shift!"

"No problem. We all have to start sometime."

"I guess so."

"There are some things you should know about this old truck. First, it is old and needs tender loving care. If the old girl decides you have not given her enough attention, she will leave you stranded in the middle of nowhere. It's best to take a horse with you on those long trips. Also, the shifter knob is off another truck and doesn't match the shifting pattern for this truck. First is here, and reverse is here. That should give you a start. Singing, the Kid put it in first, letting out the clutch, and the truck moved forward. He left it in first gear, driving the truck to where the bags of pellets were stored. It was slow going.

The bags of protein pellets were in a shed off the horse barn. The Kid was happy to do something that was physical. He continued singing a little about Rocky.

Now the Kid needed to drive the truck to fill the wooden feed bunks that were in the northwest corner of the field. There should be just enough bags to fill all the bunks. He also needed to keep track of the paper bags so that the wind didn't blow them all over the ranch. Walker would be checking the cows, and if he did not run into any problems, he would meet the Kid back at the tractor to feed the bulls.

The Kid got the old truck going in the right direction, shifted into second, and was slowly on his way to feed the yearlings. He was surprised that the old Dodge was moving. Driving a stick was not all that difficult.

Once at the gate, about half of the yearlings were at the gate pushing and shoving waiting for their pellets. The rest were playing in the field as if they were flatlander kids at a playground, running, kicking, and pushing their heads against each other.

The Kid stopped in front of the gate, chasing away the yearlings just like the dogs had done, except biting the heels, of course. When he did this, the yearlings at the gate spooked, running in the direction of the rest that were playing. He marveled at how much energy the yearlings were exhibiting. It was like a stampede with all the kicking and running. Cool!

He slowly drove the old Dodge over to the bunks. After he had emptied a few bags, the yearlings all at once came in his direction to eat, making it hard to stand on all the cow pies and urine. It was very slippery.

Next thing, the yearlings had the Kid surrounded, all the while trying to keep their distance eating pellets. He was fortunate. His size kept him from being literally run over. The scene reminded him of playing football; players were facing off against each other at the line of scrimmage to begin playing.

The yearlings seemed to be curious of the Kid, standing with noses sniffing the air and turning their heads from side to side, trying to get any clue as to what the Kid was all about.

As he filled the bunks with pellets, the Midwest flatlander Kid just couldn't resist playing with his opponents' ears or pulling their tails to get some kind of reaction, yellow penalty flag! He would walk to and from the flatbed, slipping on the cow pies and urine, carrying fifty-pound bags of pellets on each shoulder. While carrying the bags, he continued to pull tails and ears, teasing the five-hundred-pound yearlings, getting all kinds of yellow penalty flags!

After he had fed all the pellets, emptying all the bags, he couldn't help feel just a little disappointed. He liked teasing the five-hundred-pound yearlings.

As he was bundling the bags up, the five-hundred-pound yearlings seemed to feel the same about the Kid singing music. They just followed the Kid, slipping and sliding over the cow pies and urine to the old Dodge flatbed.

After securing the bags, he braced himself against the flatbed, sliding to the driver's door of the old truck. There are a few curious yearlings following him, sniffing the air while shaking their heads, kicking at each other and playing.

The Kid thought to himself that they seemed so much like flatlander kids playing that he could not resist trying to pet one. Maybe he would put his hand out with a few pellets to let the yearlings have a sniff. The yearlings backed farther off, still playing their game of trying to figure out who this Kid was who had pulled as many ears and tails as he could.

The Kid even tried to bend down to one knee, making himself smaller to see if that would help. He saw that technique on some television show once! The yearlings still would have none of it, except maybe one brave yearling. It was one that maybe was by now a little tired of the Kid pulling ears and tails.

This brave five-hundred-pound yearling made a charge at the flatlander to see if the Kid would stand his ground or run the other way. The Midwest flatlander Kid, with his football background, dodged the would-be tackler by slipping and sliding around what now had become his favorite old Dodge truck with an eight-track tape deck!

The singing flatlander, laughing, thought the yearling should leave the ranch way of life, maybe come play some football when it was time for him to go back to civilization. Now, like many things in the Kid's life, humor took over for any amount of good old common sense.

So, this is where the laughing Midwest flatlander Kid made his mistake. The Kid, having been a lineman playing football, bent down and braced one arm on one knee and one hand with knuckles on the ground, a three-point stance! He wanted to imitate the behavior of the yearlings by shaking his head from side to side.

Before the really smart Midwest flatlander football player Kid could even think about getting set, a five-hundred-pound yearling butted the Midwest flatlander Kid football player in the head. The yearling knocked the singing Kid over backward onto his new jeans, lots of yellow penalty flags and no more singing!

The flatlander sat on the ground, replaying the infraction in his head, maybe trying to see if the yellow penalty flag should be a fifteen-yarder. The yearlings, of course, looked for any sign that he might want to play some more, maybe go for the extra point.

The flatlander now was leaning against the truck, trying to clean himself off from all the manure and urine. He took off his golf cap, rubbing the top of his head. "Well, I won't do that again!" Now there was a bump starting to grow from that little hard button at the top of his golf cap that had been driven into his head. Laughing, the Kid thought he was growing a horn! He looked at himself all covered in cow manure and urine, thinking that old Buttercup was going to have a laugh!

"Now I am done playing with you guys. Go eat some pellets. Now go! I had better get through the gate and get back to feed the bulls. Paul will be waiting."

Walker was riding his horse in the direction of the bench. He had already checked the cows, watched the new calf suck to get the first milk from its mom, and stayed long enough to make sure that the new calf got the colostrum from the milk. Once that was over, the pair was in good shape.

Walker rode his horse with the dogs following from the bench.

It was the best place for the chance to view the fields and not be seen. The bench is a high, flat piece of land that is on the farthest point away from where all the feeding takes place. It sets across the creek above all the other fields. They used it in the past as a lookout to watch all the cows. It was just the right place to look after the Kid not have him know he was doing it!

The old cowboy watched as the Kid sang and played with the yearlings, filling the feed bunks, thinking, *Maybe he is having just a little too much fun!* Now the Kid was doing something a little curious. The old cowboy had seen football played on the telly, but what … The old cowboy started laughing. He told Sam and Helper the flatlander just got butted in the head!

While the old cowboy laughed, he thought, *The cook is never going to believe this! June will think I talked him into this foolishness and is for sure going to blame me!*

Walker headed his horse in the direction of home, having a difficult time trying to stop from laughing. He just kept talking to his dogs and even his horse about what he had witnessed the young singing flatlander Kid do.

The Kid was able to get back into the truck. He just sat all pillowed up for a moment, trying to get his bearings, and kept feeling the top of his head to see how big the lump was getting. Oh, how it hurt!

After he was able to put the old Dodge in gear, finding first, he felt a sense of relief that he could do that. Now the flatlander had to keep from popping the clutch. He was too quick. On the second try, he was able to limp to the gate in first gear.

After driving through the gate, he found with a little effort that he was able to hook the latch in place, leaving the yearlings all fenced in. The flatlander Kid had never been so happy to be done with anything more in his life than now. He thought he was by himself when he had been head-butted. Other than the lump on the top of his head and being somewhat covered in cow excrement, no one would ever know what had just happened.

But now he was starting to have the worst headache of his life, with his head just a-pounding! With difficulty, he was able to drive back to the ranch. He parked the truck, throwing away the empty bags. He walked to where the tractor was, bent over, and unhitched the wagon from the tractor, and it almost killed the Kid! After walking what seemed to an insurmountable distance, he was on his rodeo-bucking tractor waiting for the old cowboy.

"Now listen, Sam, Helper, let's not say anything to the Kid. He probably feels bad enough. We will just ask him how things went with the yearlings. We will just let him tell whatever story he wants."

Walker was talking to his dogs but mostly trying to compose himself, gathering his wits. The old cowboy just could not stop remembering what had just happened to the Kid just a short time ago. There the Kid was, sitting on the seat of the tractor, resting his head on his arms that were lying across the steering wheel of the tractor.

Walker looked like he was about to explode, with his eyes forward and especially not looking in the direction of the Kid. His face was red and his shoulders were shaking as he asked the Kid,

"Well, Kid, how did feeding the pellets to the yearlings go?"

With his head in his arms, he said, "Paul, you should have told me the yearlings were dangerous!"

The Kid raised his head, looking at Walker. At the top of his head was a lump the size of a silver dollar! Walker started laughing, asking the Kid what had happened to him. The Kid told his story with as much detail as he could bear. When the Kid had finished his story, he looked at Walker with his big grin, starting to laugh! They just sat there laughing, the Kid on the tractor and Walker on his horse with his dogs standing on the ground beside his horse. That was a scene that was too be repeated many times in the months to come.

Walker, the dogs, and the Kid on the tractor went into the bull pasture to feed. The flatlander was still a little shell-shocked, wanting to make up for his playing around with the head-butting yearlings. Walker was out in front with his dogs when the Kid saw the bulls coming out from the willows. The flatlander had never seen anything the size of these animals. They were huge!

As he got closer to the stack yard, the dogs cleared the path with totally different attitudes in dealing with the bulls. They were very aggressive! They just tore into those bulls, clearing a path to the stack yard.

The Kid started taking loads out to feed, with the bulls walking beside the tractor. He could not believe that their backs were as high as the fenders of the tractor! A couple of the bulls started facing off at each other, pushing with the front of their heads like the yearlings! The biggest bull had one horn that curved up, and the other horn curved to the front. He looked to be the dominant bull in the fight.

While the Kid watched the bulls fight, he could not believe the power and speed they were showing. The Flatlander started laughing at the thought of being butted in the head by one of these animals. Ouch!

"Hey, Paul, I think we should have fed the bulls first!"

"How's that, Flatlander?"

"Well, if I would have seen these big fellows fight, I could have saved myself from getting butted in the head. Looking at those two bulls fight, I would have never considered playing with the yearlings!"

"Do you think so?"

"Well yeah, look at those two go at it!"

"Yeah, those two bulls still have not figured out who is boss. They seem to fight all the time. When they are fighting like this, a flatlander has to be awfully careful. Those big fellows, as you call them, move pretty fast. If you were to get butted by them, it would be all over for you! But I would not worry about those two big fellows. You have a bigger problem!"

"I have a bigger problem?"

"Yes, you have. The cook is not going to let you in her cookhouse all covered like you rolled in cow pies and urine! If you want to eat your supper at the table and not out in the barn, you need to change your clothes. Now let's get done with feeding. A couple more loads should do it."

The Kid fed the last of the hay, and they closed up the stack yard, starting for the gate with Walker and the dogs following behind the tractor. The Kid was happy the workday was coming to a close. All he had to do is to get old Buttercup in and do the milking.

Walker made sure the Kid made it through the gate and that the gate was latched. Riding his horse, he decided to get old Buttercup out of the barn field and into the corral so the Kid could get her in to do the milking. Once the Kid was able to win the old cow's affection, he could catch the old milk cow by himself.

As the old cowboy with his dogs approached dear, sweet Buttercup, she knew there was trouble coming! The old cowboy had a look about him, one she had seen too many times before. Today he did not have the time to deal with her being cantankerous. She decided to forgo the normal late afternoon fight to be corralled. Walker by himself on foot was something to mess with. But he was with those dogs of his, riding his horse. She thought today there would be no chance in trying to escape and walked right through the gate to the two half doors at the back of the barn.

The timing could not have been better. The Kid was just starting to open the barn doors. Old Buttercup walked right into the barn, putting her head into the head catch, waiting for her oats.

"Paul, that was good timing, thanks! You were also right about June not letting me in the cookhouse. I tried to pick up the milk bucket, but she gave me that look of, 'Oh no you don't' and had me wait in the mudroom while she handed me the milk bucket."

"Did she see your head?"

"No, I had my golf cap down low over my eyes."

"Well, Kid, I am in a hurry to get done! There is a story that needs to be told to the cook that cannot wait." Walker was starting to laugh.

"Yeah, I wonder what story that could possibly be. I thought maybe we could keep that story between us."

"Kid, If I decided not to tell the cook this really great story, which, by the way, would cost me in ways that only a married man could understand, how would you explain that silver-dollar bump on your head? But there is one last thing you should know," he said, smiling that Walker smile.

"What would that be?" the Kid asked, smiling.

"However, June finds out, you can bet that the rest of the country will hear the story! People working on the ranch have very little as far as entertainment," Paul replied, smiling.

"You're telling me that I am out here to entertain the hardworking ranch folks? Maybe I had better get some oats for that dear sweet pee-kicking flatlander milk cow, Buttercup," the Kid said, laughing.

They both just continued to laugh while they went about finishing their chores.

Sam and Helper were watching the old cowboy do his normal routine at the end of the day, rubbing his horse's neck, thanking him for the good day's work. The bridle would come off next, and after that he would rub behind the horse's ears lightly, where the bridal had worn the hair with sweat. The saddle was the next item to come off, worn from all the years of riding, showing that the rider had put a lot of work into its care. Walker had a .30-30 Winchester slipped into a scabbard and a lariat on the right side hanging off the saddle horn. The saddle's stirrups had leather covers, tapadaros, to protect his feet from the weather. There were saddlebags that had all his medicine and supplies he would need to help a sick friend. There also was a yellow slicker rolled up tight and tied to the back of the saddle with a couple of square knots to hold it in place.

When the old cowboy took the saddle off, he set it on the saddle rack, placing the horse blankets on top, turning the blankets over to let the sweat dry. Then he took a soft horse brush, using it on his horse from the top of his mane to his tail. While brushing him, he checked for injuries that might have happened during the day's work. Walker would next check the horse's feet to see if the shoes were in good shape for the next day. If not, he would take the time to fix what problems there were. While all this was going on, his horse had the best grass hay to eat and the time to cool down before he turned him out for the night.

After his horse was out for the night, it was time to brush the dogs. Sam and Helper waited with great anticipation for Walker to be done with his horse. They so much looked forward to his affection after a day's work. Sam got his brushing first being the dad and lead of the two. First Paul brushed Sam's back, and then on to his belly.

Helper could hardly contain herself while her dad got his well-deserved brushing. She always tried to stay calm but would generally get to nipping at the bottoms of the old cowboy's chaps to let him know it was her turn.

When all this was completed, all three are finished for the day and then maybe they would tell a tale about a singing Midwest flatlander Kid to the cook.

"Hey Sam, Helper, do you think that old cow understands English like you two? The Kid sure does a lot of talking to that old Buttercup, doesn't he?"

"All right, my dear, sweet Buttercup, I am giving you double portion of oats. Why? Because I am a nice guy. So, let's get some rules lined out! There will be no kicking, peeing, and especially the big number two. Got that, my dear, sweet old Buttercup?" The old milk cow turned her head, looking at the Kid, who was already covered in dried cow pies and urine, with what seemed like a look of sympathy before she started in on her oats.

The Kid went to grease his hands with bag balm, finding there was a curry cob next to the tin of bag balm that was not there in the morning. He guessed that the old cowboy put it there and this was the start of his education.

The singing flatlander started to comb dear, sweet Buttercup on her back and sides, with the old milk cow enjoying all the attention. He then sat down on the stool, cleaning all the dirt from her bag and teats, putting his left leg stretched out between the old cow's back legs and the milk bucket. Leaning his head into her flank, the singing Flatlander discovered there was still a lump on his head. Ouch, damn button.

With that, Buttercup moved a little, straightening her back legs. The Kid quickly grabbed the milk bucket, standing up as fast as he could, laughing. False alarm. She was just getting a little more comfortable. There were no bowel movements.

After he had milked Buttercup and once the barn doors were latched, he was relieved that the day was finally over. He picked up his full bucket of milk starting for the cookhouse.

Walker opened the door to the mudroom with the dogs going to their respective horse blankets, either between Paul's recliner or under the chair of dispute. After hanging up all his work clothes on hooks in the mudroom, the old cowboy sat in his recliner smiling.

"Paul, you look happy. So how was the rest of the day? I could see you guys out my kitchen window laughing and having a good time. What was that all about?"

"Oh, the Kid is just excited to be doing anything on the ranch. He just never realized how fun it can be to feed yearlings is all. I guess I should be as happy as the flatlander. But I will say he has a different way of doing things!"

"Paul, what have you done to the Kid?"

"Now see, I knew you would think I had something to do with what happened!"

"Paul, you better get to telling me something before the Kid gets back from his milking!"

"Old girl, I told the Kid I would let him tell his story, so you are going to have to wait till he gets done!"

"Paul, is he all right?"

"I think that Kid probably has figured that he is not the biggest thing out here on the ranch."

"Walker what did you get him to do so you could entertain yourself?"

"Old girl, the Kid did this all by himself! I just watched with Sam and Helper, didn't we, Sam? I will say this: I have not stopped laughing. It's about the funniest thing I have ever seen!"

"Now you better tell me before he gets back! I don't want to laugh in front of him."

"Well, that train has left the station. Just be nice to the flatlander. This is only his first day, and if this is any example as to what is going to happen, we need to get this Kid to stay on longer than just the summer. I have never seen a more good-natured kid. He just is laughing and kidding all the time and seems to enjoy the hard work."

The scene was set. June, Paul, and the dogs were waiting for the Kid to finish with the milking. June had taken special care to make supper, which was stew. She just liked to cook for folks who liked to eat, and the Kid surely fit that description!

June would get the big roasting pot from the big kitchen cabinets and start the process of building the stew. There was seared venison, potatoes, carrots, peas, corn, celery, and a little bit of sweet onion slowly cooking in beef broth. She always liked to add a little flour for thickening and sweet cream for taste to the broth. The stew would cook for most of the day while she baked more sourdough bread and a couple of rhubarb pies with thick lattice so that you could see the filling spill through the little squares. Of course, to wash it done there was fresh milk.

The Kid was walking back to the cookhouse, talking to himself. "You had better be ready to come clean with your story! Because you know for sure Paul is telling June all about what happened." All the while, he adjusted his golf cap, thinking he might be able to cover the lump from view. The flatlander wondered how long the lump was going to take to go down. Probably days. "Shit, I can't hide it for days! Oh, how I hate this, and on my first day ranching! He stood at the mudroom door, pausing, and taking a deep breath, walked in.

He walked over to the sink, setting the bucket of milk on the counter, realizing he had forgotten to change his clothes. *Oh God!* He thought.

June poured the fresh milk over a strainer, letting the milk spill into a glass container. She was trying not to make eye contact with the Kid, acting like it was serious business straining milk! Once the milk was strained and put in the refrigerator, the Kid, wearing all his new clothes covered in cow pies and urine, stepped as carefully out of the cookhouse as he could to change his clothes and wash up for supper.

"Paul, there doesn't seem to be anything wrong physically with the Kid. There are no broken bones, no cuts. I didn't see any blood. So what in the world happened to the Kid that made him look like he was rolled on the ground in manure and urine?"

"So, you didn't see his head?"

"Well, I was busy pouring the milk through the strainer. You saw him; he had his golf hat pulled down on his forehead. What, did that old milk cow kick him in the head, like she did the boss? You know she broke his nose and that's why you have been doing the milking. The boss is plumb nervous to milk the old Buttercup now!"

"Really, June, you shouldn't be telling the Kid that, he'll get plumb nervous! So, let's keep that bit of information between us and let's see how the Kid gets along with the Buttercup."

The outside door to the mudroom opened, with the Kid wearing more of his new clothes stopping just short of the doorway going into the kitchen area. He was just short of where the real cowboy and the cook, two bona fide ranch folks, were waiting with all those embarrassing questions. He was just pausing at what was going to be the first of many awkward moments yet to come on his time spent ranching. He was still pausing.

June and Paul heard the Kid come into the mudroom. But the Kid hadn't said a word yet. All his three hundred pounds of hotcakes stood just short of the doorway. He looked to be thinking about something.

"Flatlander, are you going to stay out in the mudroom eating your supper?"

"Maybe, it's nice out here. Paul," he answered, smiling.

"Kid, Paul said that you had an interesting first day," June said, smiling.

The Kid's shoulders sank. He rolled his eyes to the back of his head, muttering obscenities to himself. *I just knew Paul would tell the cook!* He took the couple of steps to the doorway and gave his teacher a look of disgust. "You told June what happened?"

"Now, Flatlander, June said she would butt me on top of my head if I didn't tell her what you did that caused such a ruckus today!"

"Oh, aren't you just hysterical!"

"OK, both you two stops with the playing around and tell me what the heck happened!"

The Kid took off his hat to let the world, or at least the cook, see the silver-dollar lump he had on the top his semi-bald head, which, by the way, seemed to be getting bigger.

"Kid, what in the world did you hit your head on? You had better get over here to let me have a look at that," June said, laughing.

After the flatlander sat down, he turned his chair to have a stare-down contest with Helper under what he had already claimed as his chair.

"Haven't you had enough fun for the day? Quit staring at the dog. You know, it almost looks like you are growing a horn," she said, laughing.

The Kid began laughing while still staring at the dog.

After a minute or two, the Kid told his story. It was a story he would have to tell many more times during his time working on the ranch. The cook would just help the Midwest flatlander Kid start the rumor going to all the natives in the valley. He would have to tell the real story with all the actual details later down the road.

"What in the world would make you want to butt a yearling, of all things, in the head?"

"Thank you, but that is not what happened! I was trying to pet one, and when that did not happen, I just bent down in my three-point football stance and shook my head at the yearling. Guess the yearling thought I wanted to butt heads. Anyway, I got knocked on my butt, and now my head has this horn growing on it!"

"Well stop talking so I can get a closer look, and quit staring at the damn dog!"

June had looked at many injuries over the years of ranching. She thought the Kid probably would have a horn and headache for a while. Maybe some food would be the ticket to help heal his ego.

They all sat at the table talking about the day's events. Other than the yearling debacle, the Kid had learned a lot making his first day just fly by.

"June. I swear I cannot remember when in a day I have had the chance to eat so much good food! So, if you don't mind, I will go and settle in for the evening."

He cleaned up his dishes, thanking them both for the great day, and before leaving, paused at the table, grabbing a second piece of pie in case he was to get hungry before bedtime. That was a given!

The Kid walked back to his room and started a fire in the potbellied stove, exhausted from the day's work. The flatlander just stared at the fire through the open door, thinking of all he had done in his first day on the ranch.

The day had been long, from about 5:00 a.m. to 6:00 p.m. The total volume of information that he had learned and needed to remember was enormous!

The first thing that came to mind was he had always wanted to learn to drive a stick shift and did that on both the tractor and old Dodge pickup. When starting to drive the tractor, he had popped the clutch, with the front end of the tractor coming off the ground, popping a wheelie! The old cowboy had teased him about getting bucked off, and they both had laughed about that!

Oh, and let's not forget the dear, sweet Buttercup. That old milk cow is a load of fun with her needing her full cow massage and bathroom habits. Walker wanted him to catch her in the morning on his own, since he had gotten along with her so well on his first day. He would have to get up earlier to be able to catch her and take his time milking her, making sure there was a full bucket of milk.

Then he remembered the bulls. They were huge! He had never been that close to any animal of that size. They walked right beside the tractor. They were so close! Even as big as they were, boy could they move! And those two that fought—my God, if a person was to get in their way, it would be all over but the crying!

Now those little calves were about as cute as anything he had ever seen! They would group around a momma cow while the rest of the cows would eat. They would just run, kick, and then go for some more milk!

As he ate his pie, he thought, *Let's not forget the yearlings!* Yeah, he had embarrassed himself a little there. Paul and June teased him about playing football with the yearlings, enjoying the story from the Kid's first day. He would have to think twice before trying to scrimmage anymore with the stock animals and definitely would not bend over and shake his head at a yearling.

Then there was June and all the homemade food. It was really the best grub he had eaten in a very long time since moving west, and all he wanted. He would have to watch her so as to be able to cook for himself when he was done for the summer. Boy was the food ever good!

But the thing that stood out the most was Walker and his dogs. The old cowboy looked exactly like he had imagined from all the books and movies. He dressed the same, rode a stud horse, and had about the toughest, most ornery dogs on the planet.

Yesterday when he had arrived, what now seemed a very long time ago, he was really nervous about the move and what the new people, the natives, would be like.

The old cowboy had made him feel he was more than welcome and never seemed to get upset about anything. He just seemed to take things in stride. He was so low key! He made the Kid feel at ease being the flatlander in a valley of natives.

The Kid by this time was ready for a good night's sleep. The pot-bellied stove was set to last the night, with the damper turned almost shut. It was now time to crawl into his sleeping bag for a night's sleep or as a cowboy would say, get some shuteye.

Old Brown

While driving the old Dodge with all its added gray tape and baler twine holding all its antique broken bones together, the Kid thought maybe he was getting pretty used to the old truck by this time. Every once in a while, he would pop the clutch with the engine dying, but who cared? No one was around to watch! It was great that Paul would give him a quick run through on any chore and then turn him loose. It just made learning so much easier to be alone.

After spending his morning cleaning up stack yards, irrigation ditches, and head gates preparing for spring runoff, the Midwest flatlander Kid was a little anxious to get back to the ranch. He kept thinking the day had started the same as always, until something happened.

Carrying the empty milk bucket the short distance down the barn hallway, he let the old milk cow in the double doors. The Kid liked starting his mornings early and that his day began before anyone else's.

It had taken a lot of convincing on his part to get the old milk cow to like him. Oh, she had gone through all the normal bowel movements and even kicked the Kid a few times, emptying the milk bucket in the process. But old, dear, sweet Buttercup had taken mercy on the flatlander, and now she even waited for him at the barn door.

Once he started milking the old milk cow, a cat showed up, Ike. He assumed it was named after President Eisenhower. The cat was a minx, raw-boned, dog-eaten, milk-drinking, tough cat! Ike had six toes on her front paws and a coat that was colored black and with a white saddle. There was not one dog on the ranch, even Sam, that would try to give Ike the cat a second look. The Kid had watched more than once Ike take on a dog who wanted to see who was toughest. Ike made them all regret their rude behavior!

Nowadays the Kid's morning started with teasing the tough cat as he milked Buttercup. Ike would wait for the Kid to start to do his milking and somehow jump the closed stall gate to get her breakfast. Ike then would sit vary patiently while the Kid milked Buttercup. She knew by now the Kid liked to squirt the warm milk at her. It had become their game. He would wait until she had all but run out of patience, and then he let her have it, always laughing at how the cat opened her mouth as wide as she could, catching the milk flying her way. By the time they finished playing, Ike was drenched in warm milk! She always just sat washing her face clean with her paws while the Kid finished milking Buttercup.

The Kid was hoping maybe someday Ike would let him get close enough to pet her. But Walker had warned him that Ike did not like to be handled. The flatlander Kid took that as a challenge rather than the cautionary tale that it was intended to be. He didn't think the cat fell in the category of Walkers' working stock. Ike was a cat. How could the old cowboy train a cat to work cattle or anything else for that matter?

Since the first day of working on the ranch, he liked finding ways of becoming friends with the animals that nobody else seemed to care about or that were the toughest. It just seemed to make things interesting, given that animals on the ranch surrounded him anyway.

That's why the Midwest flatlander Kid was so excited now— another animal, a horse! This morning after milking old Buttercup and teasing Ike, the old cowboy asked him a question. "How would you like it if I were to get you a horse so you could help out with the cowboying?"

After opening the gates, the Midwest flatlander Kid sat on top of the corral, waiting for any sign that Walker, a real cowboy, was on his way. After what seemed like hours, he had to go to the barn for something to do. He was nervous! He just walked around the barn, investigating all kinds of things. He thought the loft might be a good lookout position.

Just a few minutes passed by when the sound of hooves came from a distance. The Kid looked out the big loft double doors and at a distance saw the herd of horses coming.

It was a sight to see! There was Walker with his dogs trailing what looked to be about thirty head of horses loping at an easy pace toward the corral. All seemed to be happy for the end of winter, kicking up their feet and shaking their heads. The Midwest flatlander Kid just looked at the scene trying to imagine doing the same thing.

It wasn't long before the old cowboy had the horses in the corral, shutting the gates behind. The flatlander Kid ran down the loft stairs and out of the barn as fast as he could, stepping up onto the corral poles and checking out all the horses.

"Kid, what do you think about all the horses?"

"Paul, it looked like you were having pretty good time," he answered, smiling.

"Let's take my horse to the barn, and then we will get some dinner."

Walker led his horse to water and then to the barn. Particular is a good word to describe the old cowboy's thoughtful care given to all his animals in their day working with him. When tying a horse that he was leaving for a while, he took off any headgear, tying the horse with a halter rope. When he tied his horse up, it was with a bowline knot in case the horse pulled on the halter. The knot would almost always come out.

The next thing he would do was loosen the cinch and pick up the saddle, letting air get between the horse and saddle. While he was doing this, he was looking at the horse for any problems that might have occurred in the morning's ride.

Finally, the horse always had a full manger a hay to eat while he waited for the old cowboy to come back.

Waiting to go to dinner, the Kid just watched Walker take care of his horse. It was like many things that the old cowboy did with his animals: caring, deliberate, and routinely the same every time, not wasting any time. What looked like a lot to have had to accomplish he did in no time at all.

After sitting in his chair, the Kid was preoccupied with getting his first horse and missed that Helper had not heeled him.

"So, guys, how did your mornings go?"

"The horses are in, and after dinner, the Kid will pick out his horse. How about your morning, June?"

"Paul, if we're going to town on Friday, the Kid needs to help the boss butcher tonight after supper. We are about out of meat. Other than that, the morning has been fine."

"Well, Kid, it sounds like you have your evening all lined out!"

"Paul, that's all right. How do we go about deciding which horse is going to be mine to ride?"

"By the time we finish dinner, the horses will have had a chance to settle down a bit. That might make it easier for you to look them over. Then you pick the one that best suits what you are looking for.

Nothing to it!"

"That is easy for you to say, you've been doing it your whole life. I, on the other hand, don't have a clue as to what to look for!"

"Sure, you do. Just sit there and take a minute to think it over. Give an old cowpoke a chance at the table! Come to think about it, that's a great idea! I should get a ten-minute head start all the time! By the way, Flatlander, hope you noticed that my well-behaved dog did not heel you when you sat down. Why do you think that is?"

"Maybe the milk cow had a talk with cat. The cat talked to the Helper, saying to knock off the funny business," he answered, smiling.

"Ah, there goes that Flatlander sense of humor. But I think you finally figured out how to sit in the chair and not disturb the dog. What do you think?"

"Paul, I sat down a little easier that time. I just figured that all this time she was letting me know that she was lying under the chair and for me to be careful sitting down."

"Well, I applaud your mighty frame for thinking of my dog's feelings on the matter! She has been laying there since she was a pup. Helper has picked out that spot because she feels safe under the chair and it is next to her dad. It's just polite to consider the Helper's feelings, don't you think?

After eating a quick dinner and politely excusing himself, the flatlander kid, using a hurried, long stride, was at the corral waiting for the old cowboy, looking at all the horses. Once the smiling old cowboy thought the Kid had waited enough after his leisurely dinner, he made the walk to the corral.

There, side by side, the old cowboy had a boot and the Kid had a tennis shoe on a corral pole watching the horses mingle. The Kid was looking through the corral poles trying to decide what he should be looking for; Paul had said to think about it, that he somehow knew all or some of what he wanted in a horse to ride. There were so many choices. There were different ages, colors, and sizes. He really could not understand how he could know when he had never been on a horse.

"So have you arrived at a choice?"

"Paul, I do not have a clue."

"Let's go at it this way. We have about thirty horses to choose from. What would be the first thing you would need to consider?"

"Me and how big I am."

"Yes, good choice. By the way, how much do you weigh?"

"More now than I did on my first day! I would guess close to three hundred, give or take a hotcake or two!"

"Yeah, the cook does a pretty good job. Think I'll keep her. Yes, weight is surely something to consider. But think of this, not to be disrespectful. You do not have a clue how to ride a horse. You need to be looking for a horse that you will be able to learn from. That horse has to have been already educated from being handled and ridden. That rider has taught that horse his way of communication of having a rider on his back.

"The problem most people have at this point is they don't match the animal to their experience and personality. For instance, a person who has little to no experience picks a horse that is green broke. How much chance do you think that person has of getting along with that horse? Not much. Let's get worse—a person who has little time to invest in the animal, always in a hurry, expects the horse to act on every instruction that he gives. That's a big problem!

"So now you have to pick a horse that will be able to teach you the skills of how to ride. You have to have the time and patience to listen. Take the time to care about the animal that knows more than you do. Describe that horse to me, and look at the horses when you give me that description."

"Well kind of like you, someone who has some age, experience, knowledge, skill, and above all, patience," he said, smiling.

"You kind of scared me there! But yes, you are right, especially about patience—a lot of patience," the cowboy answered, smiling. "Let's throw in a sense of humor. That always helps! How about gelding or mare, does that matter?"

"I don't think I should be riding a stud like you. Probably a gelding or a mare that is not dominant in the bunch. Wait a minute—I do not see any other studs in the corral, but you ride a stud. How is that? "

"I would not be riding a stud if there was one in the corral, would I?"

"That has to help you with the rest of the horses because you ride the dominant one in the bunch!"

"Yes, that is correct. Now how old do you think a horse should be before a person starts to ride him?"

"I'll use my physical fitness training to answer that, the age when the animal is almost or is done growing."

"I'll give you that. If given the chance, I like to start handling the foal as soon as it has mothered up. The reason for that is to get the foal used to me being the lead in front of its mother. It helps establish dominance in a good way. There really doesn't need to be any forcing the issue of dominance when they are that young. By doing it this way, it is natural to the foal. The foal sees me handle its mother, and it is just logical for the foal to except me as lead.

"But I don't always get that chance when they are that young. When I work with a young horse, a two-year-old that's already been away from its mother for awhile, I'll put my stud with the young horse to let them get acquainted, letting my horse begin to buddy up. After I see that the younger horse as accepted the stud has his dominant influence, I then start to work the younger horse from the stud. Since I am riding the natural lead to the younger horse, the stud, it makes me the lead to the younger horse.

"Once the younger horse is used to me handling it from the stud and on foot, I then put an empty saddle on its back for the initial weight, taking it on short trips trailing behind me riding the stud.

"I continue that process till the younger horse is about three years of age. Then I start the process of putting a rider's weight on their backs. Now I am guessing that I weigh only about hundred and fifty pounds. In combination with the saddle's weight, I am able to start riding the horse for short periods of time. There's no tough riding, probably only walking and teaching. I start to work them harder after bridle teeth have come in, about the age of five.

"So we are down to what, able to carry a large load of hotcakes, no green broke horses, and age now has become a factor. When you make your choice, look for a horse that likes to be handled by you, and match your personalities. In your case, find a horse that likes to listen to you talk and be petted a lot," he said, smiling.

"Now I am going to get my horse, and we are going to cut out the horses that are out of the running. I would bet you could make a choice or two after that.

"I'll need you to operate the gate. When you see me haze a horse against the corral fence, open the gate and let the animal through. If there are any problems, just shut the gate, and we will start again."

That is how it worked. Walker worked the horses through the gate to where there was only about half left. The ones left seemed to settle down a bit. Walker rode over to the Kid.

"Taking those horses out might make it easier. Do you have any choices yet?"

"I like the old brown gelding."

"You made a good choice. He has had many years working cattle in the mountains. Here, I have a halter and brush for you. Get acquainted. I'm going to catch a couple of horses for cow camp and turn the rest out. Come see me in the barn when you get done."

The brown gelding was a big horse of almost seventeen hands with a white blaze on his nose.

"I can already tell from the start, you are a lot easier to get along with than old Buttercup. We had a problem of her wanting to have multiple bowel movements and then there was the kicking! You're a horse. How in the heck can a cow kick the Kid milking and the bucket over at the same time?"

Slow and easy, the Kid brushed the old brown horse from the forelock to his tail while making the horse stand quiet until he was done.

The Kid walked brown to the barn, where Walker was brushing one of the cow camp horses. The other horse was tied to a post on the outside of a stall and standing in the barn hallway.

"Paul, I like this old brown."

"You made a good choice. You'll be able to learn what you need from the old brown."

"How do I go about that?"

"I think respect is the first thought that comes to mind. It doesn't matter if you are learning from a person like myself or a horse. We have been doing what you want to learn for a long time. It has taken us years to get to this point of where we are in the learning curve, and that education always comes with a heavy price. We want to pass on our knowledge to individuals like you who want to learn. All we want is for you to respect the sacrifices that were made by those who have already gone through it. You are benefiting by being taught by folks who have already made the mistakes you would make if not for them teaching you. So I want you always to be respectful of not just myself but also the animals that you will be in contact with.

"Let me go back to your question, how do you go about learning from old Brown? I think you have to become friends first. After you have been around horses for a time, you will notice that when horses meet for the first time, they groom each other. Grooming is a sign of friendship. That's why I had you curry comb the old brown out in the corral. You should always become friends before you ask an animal to do something for you, wouldn't you say? That is what we are going to do all afternoon with the horses, make friends.

"We are now going to check out old Brown's feet. Again, when holding a halter rope, squeeze the coils in your hand. Don't hold them in a coil wrapped around your fingers. You hold the old brown, and I will show you how to put shoes on the horse."

Walker bent down, lifting one of the horse's feet so that the hoof came up from behind and between his legs so that the hoof was face up to allow Walker to work on it. He went through all the terms the Kid should become familiar with—the frog, the quick. Then it was the tools, rasp, clinchers, horse pick, pull off, driving hammer, and anvil. Horseshoes were next and nails with only one way to be hammered.

Next the Kid watched Walker trim and take the rasp to the hoof. He made it look so easy. When the hoof was done, it looked like it had been to a pedicurist. The Kid was so impressed with the old brown. He just stood while the old cowboy was putting shoes on him.

The Kid just stayed quiet, watching with keen interest. There was a lot to remember, and he wanted to able to do his best when it was his turn.

"Now let me show you where and how to tie the old brown in a stall. To tie a horse up, I want you to use a bowline knot like this. I'll find you a piece of rope to practice with before we go to supper. You want to tie him short. By this, I mean so he stays put in the stall, just enough so he can reach the hay toward the bottom of the manger. This old horse has been through a lot today; let's show him how good he has been! Let's use this stall. The manger is full of good hay, and let's get some oats—one coffee can if you would. Now let's shoe the other two horses."

Walker and the Kid worked together putting shoes on the other two horses. The horses were not as big as the old brown and were not as easy either! More than once, the old cowboy and the Kid had to take a break.

"Well, how are you doing?"

"Good I think."

"I hope we didn't wear you out. There is the butchering yet to do after supper."

"I will be fine. Do you want these horses tied up as was done with the brown?"

"That would be great if you would. After you get done with that, the brown can be let loose out the side door. Let me show you. See how the bowline just comes out, no effort at all. Open the barn door just enough like so, and here is the trick: loop the halter rope around his neck near his ears, giving the rope a couple of light tugs. That lets the old brown know you have him by the halter rope. While holding the halter rope around his neck, unhook the halter. You still have your horse. Thank him for his good day's work by rubbing his neck, slowly letting the halter rope go from around his neck. See, he still believes his is held!

"I have seen too many people just unhook the halter. The horse gets to thinking that is the signal that the day is done. Many horses will break away from the person. Sometimes things can go wrong, getting someone hurt.

"We will leave these two horses in the barn so they can finish eating. I'll turn them loose after supper."

The cook and the old cowboy spent their supper teasing the Kid that maybe he should not have named the grained two-year-old steers in the back of the barn that were to be butchered. Everyone had laughed at his impending loss of a family member, Butkus, named after his favorite football player. Not long after that, the boss showed up to get the Kid's help to butcher his favorite middle line backer from his favorite football team, da Bears.

Again, smiling to himself about the flatlander Kid, the old cowboy walked to the barn with both his dogs grabbing at his pant cuffs, a game he had played with them from the beginning. Walker believed that when working with animals, you had to be boss of them. But also, there was time for play after the dogs had earned their keep. It was a matter of timing and balance so as not to turn the animal into a pet. That was something the Kid was going to have to learn. Animals were wonderful companions and friends, but you have to give a dog or horse a job to do. It makes them feel that they are contributing to the whole, the pack. Once they do the job, it is then fine to play a little.

The dogs were anxious to getting their much-deserved brushing. It was the routine the old cowboy used from the beginning. That was something else that the Kid needed to understand: animals liked routine. It gave them a sense of dependency on the lead, nothing more than parents providing for their children. Children need to have the guarantee of home and above all affection that they are a trusted part of the whole.

Walker enjoyed this time of day. He liked being by himself in the barn, just taking his time to finish out the day with his animals. The barn was a great place to do some odds and ends and puttering.

"You two seem to have finished your oats. Let's turn you out so I can brush the dogs. The Kid tied a pretty good bowline for you. He seems to catch on to what needs to be done. Thanks for the good day. Now be gone with you. I can't stay here at the door all night scratching your ears. Now go on get out there and say hello to the old brown. The old devil has a lot of work ahead of him!

"OK, you're next. Thanks for being patient. The knot the Kid tied looks a little chewed. What do you think about that? It always seems to me that the smart ones always give me the problems! Yeah, I'm a trying. Don't be in such a hurry, young fellow, I taught you better than that!

"Now stand there for a bit till you decide to behave. You are going to cow camp. I am going to use you to pack all my food and belongings around the country for the summer. But this summer we have the Kid with us. At times, you are going to get a little more to carry—mostly food. That Kid can eat a bunch," he said, smiling. "We want to get him in the high country so he can have something to talk about and remember when he goes back to the city.

"See, all you needed was a little time to remember who's boss. There you go. Visit with those other two so I can give Sam and his daughter some attention.

"Did you think I forgot you two? Come here to get your brushing. Helper, hold on there, wait your turn! Your dad gets his first. You need to be a little more patient. Do you like that, Sam? How about I brush your tummy? You know that girl of yours is nipping at my pant cuffs. One day she is going to pull me over. Yeah, yeah, all right, girl. You just cannot wait your turn.

Yea, I bet it feels good. There, we are done! Now let's go to the cookhouse and get another small piece of pie.

While the old cowboy was walking back to the cookhouse, he heard the sound from a small caliber handgun. Farewell to Butkus, the flatlander's favorite middle linebacker steer!

Breakfast and Town

The Kid got up at his normal time of 5:00 a.m. to milk the old milk cow and visit with his two friends. He was anxious to tell old Buttercup what he did last night after supper. The Kid was giving the old milk cow her morning massage, just talking away, asking all kind of questions.

"Buttercup, I do have a question for you. What in the world do they do with all the internal organs from Butkus? The boss had me cut out the heart, tongue, liver, and oh my God, the damn brains. What could they possibly do with the brains? Probably the Sam and Helper get the chance to eat those delicacies, what do you think?"

While the Kid is milking dear, sweet Buttercup, Paul and June were enjoying their early morning, talking and laughing at how the Kid's face had looked when he brought Butkus' internal organs in the cookhouse the previous night.

"Now June, I think the Kid has got to have the best sense of humor I have been around. Look how the Kid got butted in the head by, of all things, a yearling. He just laughed it off. Heck, it would have killed most people. This Kid is some of the best entertainment I have ever been around. I do not think my life is going to ever be the same."

"I have to admit, the Kid does some funny things. OK, Paul, here the Kid is coming, now take it easy."

"Good morning! Old Buttercup was at the door again, and now that pregnant cat meets me there. Paul, I think this old flatlander is doing pretty good with the milk cow. Pretty soon I think it should be time for me to try something a little more difficult," he said, smiling.

"Well it sounds like ranch life is agreeing with you. You have trained two of the toughest critters on the ranch, a milk cow and a cat," he said, smiling. "Maybe let old Brown take you to the point of something more your size. Maybe try playing a little football with the old war pony."

"OK, you two stop with the playing around. All of us have a long day ahead, and I need to get things ready for the trip to town. So now get up to the table and eat some breakfast," she said, almost laughing.

"Kid I will give you a head start on eating scrambled eggs and toast," Walker said, smiling. "I will just sit here in my big recliner watching the show as you devour another meal. By the way, Kid, how the heck hungry are you this morning? I am just saying with you working a long day yesterday doing the butchering, you should eat all that you want."

"Paul, thanks, you know that's right, I did work late, and I am a little more hungry than normal. The scrambled eggs look really good! Do you have a little syrup I can put on top? That makes the sausage taste sweet."

"You know, Kid, I feel bad that I have been teasing you like I have. We have the time for you to take another helping, so take all the time you want. Let's finally see if we can fill your bulk up. Eat all you want."

Now the Kid gave the old cowboy a questioning eye, as if to say, "What are you up to this time?" But that is indeed what the Kid did. Paul and June were just watching with big smiles on their faces, almost to the point of bursting, Paul could hardly contain himself.

"You know, Kid, I have just one question. You said you were eating sausage and eggs, right?"

"Yeah, Paul, that is what I said. Why, isn't this sausage and eggs?"

"What did you do last night after supper?"

"I helped the boss butcher a dear friend of mine, Butkus, the two-year-old steer. Why?"

"What did you bring in the bucket and give to June?

"Well, all of the internal organs. And by the way, what in the world do you do with that stuff?"

Paul and June just looked at the Kid, laughing. "What in the world are you two going on about?"

"Flatlander, you have just finished eating your second helping of brains and eggs!"

"Yeah, sure. Paul, you are not going to make me think I just ate cow brains! I would have tasted them anyway."

"Kid, brains are what you just ate. They are mixed in with the scrambled eggs you have been eating!"

"June, that cannot be. Why would anybody eat cow brains?"

Paul and June were laughing at the expression on the Kid's face. Even the dogs got off their blankets, looking at the flatlander. The Kid just sat there staring at his plate in disbelief, not knowing what to do. A couple of thoughts were running through his mind—throw up or get a little more, because it was pretty good eating!

It was just the visualization of cracking skull open with a hatchet and then scooping the brains out with his bare hands that made him a little queasy. He had been so careful to lay them in the bucket with rest of internal organs.

"Flatlander, you don't look so good!"

"Paul, I just have one question."

"Just one question, Flatlander?"

"If that was brains and eggs, and I am not saying it was, because, Paul, I would not put it past you guys trying to play a joke on the flatlander for a good laugh, my question is this: what do you do with the rest of internal organs? By the way, Butkus probably sacrificed his life so you two could have a laugh!"

"Well, Kid, we are going to have heart and tongue for dinner! Then for supper liver and onions is on the menu," Paul answered, laughing.

"Yeah! Yeah! Now I know you are teasing me, Paul! Nobody is going to eat a heart and oh my God of all things a tongue for a meal!

"Now I am done watching you two mess around with each other! We all have a lot to do today if we are going to town tomorrow. So get out of my cookhouse, and take those ornery dogs with you!"

"Hey, Flatlander, how did you like brains?"

"Yeah, yeah, we will see, Paul! I'll wait till dinner time to say I am a believer."

Walker and the Kid were in the barn getting ready to catch the horses. The morning's humor was still leaving smiles on their faces.

The old cowboy was taking the morning to teach the Kid how to saddle his horse. What type of bridle was best for the old brown? He was somewhat concerned that the Hotcake Kid would be too big for the saddle he had chosen. It has the biggest seat of all the saddles on the ranch. That would be the choice, small or not.

The horses seemed to know that it was time for their day to start. Old Brown was at the barn door, sticking his big head over the half door with the other two horses right behind Old Brown waiting their turn.

"Look, Paul, the old brown is at the barn door. He must have watched the Buttercup and Ike early this morning deciding to do the same," the Kid said, smiling.

"Hey, Flatlander, before you get all caught up with yourself, just open the barn doors and let the horses in, would you?"

The Kid did just that. The horses came in. Old Brown was first, then the mare, and the young gelding was last. The horses walked to what seemed to be their respective stalls. Walker had already put a couple cans of oats into each of their feed bunks; the old cowboy looked at the Kid and winked.

"OK, how did you get the horses to do that?"

"You were standing right beside me! You saw I didn't do anything," Paul answered, smiling.

"Now I need you to halter Old Brown, and I will halter the other two. Tie Old Brown short with a bowline. I will let them eat while I show you some saddles and tack."

The Kid entered a small room with numerous saddles and blankets sitting on saddletrees around the tack room. On the wall across from the saddles were as many different types of bridles as there are. Among the bridles were ropes and halters.

The Kid walked out of the barn carrying his saddle over his shoulder, just like in the movies, with Walker right behind, hanging the saddle and tack on the hitching post outside the corral.

"Now go get Old Brown and bring him here. We will see if I can remember how to saddle a horse."

The Kid led Old Brown out of the barn, tying him to the hitching post. Next, the Kid started to brush Old Brown from his ears to his tail.

Then Walker went through how to saddle the old horse. "Lay the pad on Old Brown's back, and then the blanket on top of that. The saddle goes on top of the blanket, evening everything up. There is a front and back cinch; you cinch the front first, and then the back. The bridle is next, or in this case a hackamore or noseband. The hackamore goes over Old Brown's nose first, and then up over his ears.

"Now before you try to get on, walk Old Brown in a circle a couple of times. He likes to hold his breath after he has been cinched. You should always take a few steps with any horse, checking to see if you need to tighten the cinches again. There you go, Kid. Now get on Old Brown and see if the saddle fits."

The Kid remembered how Walker got onto his horse and did the same. After all the books and after all the movies, the Midwest flatlander was sitting in the saddle. The Kid was surprised at how high he was and how much of a step it was to get his foot into the stirrup and then swing his other leg over the saddle. Walker led Old Brown to the corral they were in yesterday sorting horses.

"We will go check on the pairs, seeing if you like riding the old war pony. Until you get familiar with riding and all the mechanics of communicating to Old Brown, the hackamore is the best headgear to learn from. It gives Old Brown more control than you; remember, Old Brown is teaching you! I want you to be aware of what he is telling you. I am going to saddle my horses; you two get acquainted in the corral."

The old cowboy came out of the barn, leading the mare and young gelding. The young gelding had a packsaddle rigging with no weight of any load. Walker opened the corral gate, leading the Kid riding Old Brown out of the corral, stepping into the stirrup on the mare.

Walker thought it would be a good morning to take along the Kid for a ride, since he had finished with the stack yards and clearing away debris from the irrigation ditches and head gates.

He wasn't testing the Kid by any means, but if he was to have a chance to work with him at cow camp, the Kid had to get his work done! Also, the old cowboy wanted to see what the Kid's abilities were in riding horses. The Kid had already showed gentleness with the animals he had already come into contact with. That in itself was nice to see. Now he had to show some sign as to whether he could take it to the next step. There was still time to teach him how to ride and take care of a horse. But the Kid had to show some sign he had a little natural ability.

In the past, Walker had always wanted to be at cow camp by himself. It was the only time he had to work with his stock animals without interruptions. Even to consider the idea of having someone else was new to the old cowboy. But since his stroke, he would just feel better to have someone along to help out on part-time basics. The old cowboy just had thoughts of his mortality since the stroke, thinking he should pass on some of his knowledge before he died. Besides, Walker could not remember enjoying anyone's company so much! The Kid just had a good-natured quality that Walker liked. "Kid, you ready to do a little riding?"

"You bet I am! Let's get after it," he said, smiling from ear to ear.

"We are going to ride to the upper portion of the ranch where all the runoff water starts. The ride will give you a chance to get to know Old Brown and learn a little more about the lay of the land. Since we are on horseback, I might as well show you the rest of the irrigation head gates and where the gates throw the spring runoff.

"Once we get to the upper portion of the ranch, we will follow the main creek back to the home place. It will allow us to check the pairs and the head-butting yearlings you like so well. How are you getting along with Old Brown?"

"I am doing fine. You might want to ask Old Brown that question in a few hours."

"Well, Kid, Old Brown has carried many a load. Besides, that old war pony will buck a little if you give him the chance," Paul said, smiling.

"You are trying to get me nervous. This old horse isn't going to buck, is it?"

"Kid, trust the old cowboy!"

"Paul, is there anything I should know about riding?"

"Yes, stay on top of the horse, just like the tractor," Paul replied, smiling.

"Great, that is your best advice? Come on; tell me some of your technique. You look so at ease!"

"Well, I can tell you all the technical advice that you would want. There really is no better way of learning than to ride. But you keep watching. Maybe I can show you a thing or two!"

That is how the morning went. They rode their horses to the upper portion of the ranch. Walker explained how to flood-irrigate, cycling water from one place to another. The water was only to stay on the portion of land until it was wet about three inches down. Once that happens, change the direction of the water to another area until everything has been flooded.

As golden eagles watched their every move, the two cowboys came across many different signs of wildlife: tracks from moose, mule deer, and of course, coyotes! The Kid even heard some coyotes talking back and forth in the distance.

"Paul, do you think there are any fish in that creek?"

"I would hope so. The cook hasn't caught them all yet! There are probably one or two rainbows, brookies, and even a brown trout in that creek. Have you ever done any fishing?"

"Not any out here in Montana. I did a little fishing where I grew up, but not a whole lot."

"When we go to town, you better buy a fishing pole. And let me give you some advice. The cook takes her fishing seriously! Any chance she gets, she is out fishing. It is a wonder there are any fish in the creek. If you want someone to help you buy a fishing pole, the cook is the one. But don't ask her to teach you how! The cook gets a little protective about her secret ways of fishing. She won't even let me get close to her while she is at the creek."

"Oh, come on. You're telling me that June has a secret to fishing?"

"I think there is more than one," Paul answered, smiling. "Flatlander, you ask her when she is helping you buy a fishing pole."

"Hey, Paul, what is that over there?"

"That's a beaver dam. They like to build their dams where there is deep water and plenty to eat. I will have to come back sometime soon to blow it up. You will have a heck of time spreading water with that there!"

"What do you mean blow it up?"

"I get some dynamite, come back, and blow it up."

"Cool! I'd like to learn to use dynamite," the Kid said, smiling.

"Well, I think you should work on learning to ride Old Brown first. I think I will save the dynamite for another time," Paul replied, smiling.

"You know, you are going to have to forget about the head butting some time," the Kid said, smiling.

"Maybe, but for now I do not believe you would be the one I would want carrying around dynamite anywhere near the stock," Paul answered, laughing.

They rode the rest of the morning until it was time for dinner. They took care of their horses' needs in the barn and walked to the cookhouse for dinner.

Cookie had taken particular care to arrange the meal as if it were a special occasion, like Thanksgiving! She wanted it to look like a feast for a flatlander who had butchered for the first time! The cook had laughed all morning just thinking of the reaction the Midwest flatlander Kid would have. Her laughing got to the point that she hoped no one would walk in on her, thinking that maybe she was just a *little crazy!*

Walker and the Kid went through their normal routine of hanging up coats and washing up. As it was also customary, the Kid would sit in his chair with the greatest of care, so as to not disturb the beast from down below.

Walker and the Kid had not noticed the cook looking at them both, smiling and on the brink of laughing. They were going over what needed to be done for the afternoon. After dinner, they would follow the creek all the way down to the north end of the ranch at the red butte. It would give Walker the time to show the Kid the rest of the head gates and more of the ranch. They were both looking forward to riding together for the rest of the day.

"Come on, you two, come get some dinner. I thought it would be nice to celebrate the Kid riding a horse for the first time! So get up to the table and see what I have made for the Kid," she said, almost laughing.

The Kid stood up very slowly as the routine was now, taking the few steps to the table to see the wonderfully laid out feast. The two cowboys sat at the table, looking at all the trouble the cook had gone through.

"Wow! June, you did not need to go to all this trouble just for me!"

"Well, Kid, Paul and I are happy you're here having a good time. We thought a celebration would be in order after having worked your first month and tomorrow we go to town to cash your first check. I thought it would be nice to celebrate a little!"

Paul handed the Kid the silver-covered platter of Butkus' internal organs with his ever-present really big smile!

The Kid sat the platter down in the middle of the table, taking off the silver cover. To his horror, there on the silver platter lay the heart and tongue he had cut out of his friend the two-year-old steer the night before! June and

Paul just smiled at each other, waiting for his reaction. But he just kept staring at the heart and tongue in disbelief with huge eyes and mouth agape!

"June, you have outdone yourself this time. To my recollection, I have never seen a heart and tongue on a silver platter quite like that; it looks natural like," Paul said, smiling again the Walker smile.

"Thanks, Paul, I worked most of the morning to make things look good as I could. I wanted to show the Kid how much we like having him here. It took me forever to polish the silver platter and its cover. Not to mention how careful I was in cutting up and laying out the heart and tongue!"

The Kid looked from the silver platter of his friend's internal organs, first to the cook and then the old cowboy with a look of disgust, shaking his head. Then the Kid spoke.

"I do not know what to say. Yes, I do, I am working around cannibals! You raise the damn animals around the ranch so you can eat their internal organs! No wonder the stock around here are so much on the fight! They know what is going to happen to their innards! If you think I am going to eat anything that resembles a heart and oh my God, you have got the tongue laid out like I could use it to lick a stamp!"

That was the final straw. All three just started laughing. Even the dogs came to see what was going on. Walker picked up the silver platter of internal organs, handing it to the Kid.

"You get first pick as to what looks the best," he said, smiling that Walker smile!

The Kid just held the platter in front of him, shaking his head. June had a feeling that would be his reaction and had placed jars of peanut butter and jelly on the table for plan B. From then on, the jars would be there on the table in case the Kid would object to any and all cannibal tendencies on the ranch.

The day had been rich in sentiment for the flatlander kid from the Midwest! The lay of the land was just what he had imagined, Western. The Rocky Mountains were there in the background, thick with a forest of pine trees and the valley, prairie with willows, and sagebrush looking not unlike any dream he had from childhood. While always imagining what it would be like, the Midwest flatlander Kid was riding his first horse side by side with what had to be the real deal, Walker and his cow dogs.

The two cowboys were following the main creek, investigating all possible signs that might give a clue as to what wild animals might be close by. The Kid watched how the old cowboy related to his horse. The stud somehow received information as to where to go with no words and no perceptible body signals. The horse just seemed to know where he was going!

Then the Kid watched the old cowboy's dogs that were always at his horse's side. He somehow let them know that it was time to do what needed to be done. Sam and Helper were probably the toughest of all the animals the Kid had been around, maybe except for the Ike the cat! The dogs were fearless in wanting to do what the old cowboy wanted, it just simply did not matter what! The miles the dogs covered in a day were unbelievable; they just seemed to have a wealth of energy for the entire day.

The Kid was getting a good introduction into the way of life on a western ranch for a little over a month now. It had been a change in his life that would last for the rest of his years. The thing he would remember first and most of all was the characteristic of a good-natured sense of humor. The folks teased without any hint of malice, making all the hours and days of hard work entertaining, to say the least. Then the work wasn't just from after breakfast and until supper. The work lasted as long as the work took to get done on any given day. And last, you do not waste anything when you butcher a cow for beef, even if that meant eating brains out of a steer that was named after one of your childhood sports heroes!

It was a way of life that was not about monetary gains or even waiting for the week to end so that you could spend the weekend enjoying yourself. It was a way of life that you chose because it was what you wanted to do all the time. That in itself made the long hours and the hardship worth the risk of health and monetary hardship!

This information, or you might say a realization, was not what the Kid expected or been taught his life was about. The life he was raised in was very different. It was about things you acquired and mostly how much money you could make to buy material things that you wanted. The ranch life was about surviving each day and looking forward to doing it again the next!

"Well, Flatlander, you have your first day riding under your belt. How does it feel?"

"Let me get down so I can see if I walk with the Duke's 'Howdy Pilgrim' in my step. I think if I were to spend a little more time in the saddle riding like you have for forty years, my butt would not be as numb. Other than that, I am fine and had a great time! Thanks for all your help, especially not making me eat heart and tongue," he said, smiling.

"There are no thanks necessary. You now can ride Old Brown when you think you have the need for the old war pony. A lot of the irrigation can be done riding Old Brown. Just pack a shovel when you go. It will give you time on a horse's back. And I think you have made a good choice for yourself in Old Brown."

"You are telling me I can ride Old Brown when I irrigate?"

"You bet I am! Once you get the water spread over the fields, riding a horse is the only way, other than afoot. I just frown on walking myself when there are perfectly good horses to ride. Tomorrow, we go to town; you can buy what you think you should have to ride with. I would start with a pair of cowboy boots and hat. You are a cowboy now! So, the tennis shoes and golf cap can be used for other occasions," he said, smiling just a little.

Walker and the Kid took care of their horses. The dogs were getting their brushing, and the Kid went to get the milk bucket.

The Kid was excited to know he could ride Old Brown to do the irrigating. That meant he could learn to ride by himself! Then after the trip to town tomorrow, he would look more the part of a real cowboy, leaving all his new Midwest clothes for another time.

The old cowboy and the cook were looking forward to the time away from the ranch. It had been a long few weeks for June since she had been to town buying groceries. But Paul hadn't had any time off for almost six months. That normally wasn't hard for him. It was just with having a stroke the past year, it was getting to be a load. The Kid not only helped with the humor at the ranch, but he also took a lot of the pressure off the old cowboy and the worry from the cook's mind. The drive to town allowed the three to talk of things not related to work.

"You know, June, you are killing me with those cigarettes!"

"Kid, would you rather walk the rest of the way?"

"Flatlander, you best not mess with the cook and her smoking! So tell us how you decided to work on a ranch."

"Paul, you know most of it. I came out west with a friend and decided to live here. I had spent about a year and half working for the forest service. A girlfriend of mine, Nan, cut out a help-wanted ad from the newspaper, ranch hand for hire. I had it for a long time and finally called the number. The boss answered the phone and decided to hire me from that conversation. That's the short version."

"But Kid, how did you not talk about wages?"

"Well, June, it was like this. The boss, after just a few minutes, cut the conversation off. He then started by saying that since I was from the Midwest, I probably couldn't handle the work and couldn't handle the lifestyle. By now, you have noticed I am a fairly goodsized kid. I got a little wolfy!"

"Did you tell him how big you are?"

"How big I am and how much food I eat—no, I didn't tell him that, Paul. I told him that I would work for him a month and if I did not work out, to send me down the road! The ranch would only be out room and board. If he did decide to keep me on, then he should pay me what I am worth and I would work for the whole summer, maybe longer. A really great deal for me was in my thoughts. I would get a chance to work on a ranch for at least a month. If it did not work out, I would go and hitch back up with Nan."

"That's why you really didn't care what the amount of your check was!"

"June, by giving me that check, this Kid from the Midwest was worth his wages and I could work as long as a wanted! I have to admit, I am a little surprised that the check is for only this much! But I'll bet it's probably enough for clothes."

"Kid, who is this Nan?" "June, leave the Kid alone." "Paul, I don't mind. Nan is just this really good friend that I am close to. If she had not given me that want ad, all this would not have happened. Like I said, I am having the time of my life! But enough about me, what are your stories?" "Paul and I have known each other for quiet a spell. We just have been married for last few years. My family are natives of the area. Paul has been at the ranch since the boss's grandfather, that's about forty or so years." "Wow, Paul, that is a long time to work at the same place. What was it like back then?" "Kid, it was more open and not so many fences. I hitched up with the boss's grandfather when I was about your age. That was a tough old man! You didn't have all the modern conveniences back then. Heat, water, clothes, and food were what you would expect for the thirties. The thing I seem to miss the most is working with horses more! Everything was done with horses, from riding to haying to feeding in the winter. It was just a lot tougher, a better pace with the horses."

"Paul, where did you grow up?"

"Kid, I grew up on a reservation in the eastern Dakotas. I just somehow drifted out here for work."

"What do you mean reservation?"

"Kid, an Indian reservation, I am part native Sioux Indian."

"Really, Paul, you were raised on a reservation in the Dakotas?"

"Yes. What are you surprised at, that you are working with a part Indian?"

"Well no, that is really cool! I am just wondering if the Dakotas are in the Midwest. You know if that is true, there are two flatlanders in the station wagon," he said, laughing.

"You know, Paul, the Kid has a point," June said, smiling.

"You keep smoking those cigarettes and drive," Paul replied and smiled.

"Paul, no wonder we get along so well! We are both from the same part of the country! Hey there, Flatlander!"

"OK, you two, we are about to town. I have some errands to run. You two try to stay out of trouble! But I do not think this town is ready for two Flatlanders at the same time," June said, laughing.

The cook dropped her two children off at the bank like any other mother, hoping that they would behave themselves.

"OK, Kid, we're here; let's spend all your hard-earned cash!"

"Who was that you were talking to at the bank, if you don't mind me asking?"

"That was the banker himself. He has always wanted to buy a ranch in the valley and wanted to know if I knew anything about it. But hey, we are here to spend your hard-earned money! I am wondering what size foot you have. Sasquatch."

The first two articles of clothing the Kid bought were a pair of cowboy boots and hat. The cook's oldest son, Paul, smiled, thinking he would tell his kid brother how to break the boots when the time was right, like now, for instance. "Now that I have bought my cowboy boots, what is the secret to breaking them in?"

"Kid, there really isn't much of a secret to it," Paul replied, smiling that older brother smile.

"So, Paul, how do I do it?"

"Kid, you need to put on your brand-new, expensive boots and walk in the creek; it breaks them in," he answered, smiling.

"Oh come on, Paul, how can that break my boots? They'll get wet!"

"Kid, that's the whole point! After your boots are wet, then you wear them till they dry. It makes them fit better."

"I wear them wet? That could take a while!"

"A couple of days, I would imagine."

"What do I do at night when I go to bed?"

"You sleep with them on." "You want I should sleep with my boots on?"

"Yep. Trust the old cowboy, Kid; it will make them fit like a glove!"

"Paul, is this for real? Maybe you want to play another joke on the Kid."

"Trust the old cowboy, Kid, it works!"

The next things on the Kid's list of things to buy were a pair of chaps and a fishing pole. Paul thought since his younger kid brother was so big, he might need to go to the saddle shop to have the chaps made.

While walking to the saddle shop, the older brother pulled out his chewing tobacco, grabbing a big pinch and then stuffing it in his mouth. The Kid had always been curious about how it tasted.

"Paul, is that chewing tobacco any good?"

Smiling out of some obnoxious traditional older brother affection, the older brother opened his tobacco pouch, offering his kid brother a pinch. Out of the same older brother intolerable affection, he showed his kid brother how to grab a pinch and how to put it in his mouth so that he was still able to spit, or if he wanted to be a real cowboy, he should just swallow. The sadistic older brother had his kid brother go back to the pouch, getting a bigger pinch.

Once the Kid brother had his really big chaw in place, his older brother had a look of satisfaction on his face, or was it a look of winning just one more time, as all older brothers have? He just watched as his kid brother's face showed different expressions: from smiling to getting red faced to sweating profusely. They walked for a little while, and Paul knew his kid brother was having some real concerns by this time. They had almost made it to the saddle shop when his kid brother made the most awful sounds of gagging and coughing. It was hard at the time to distinguish which one was happening.

"This chaw is burning the heck out of my mouth! Why in the world do you put this stuff in your mouth?"

"I believe it is an acquired taste. Hey there, you shouldn't spit it out on the ground. That's about half my pouch of chewing tobacco!"

"I would be glad to put it back, if you want."

"No. I have had my fun with you," Paul answered, smiling that big brother smile. "But if you have any money left, you owe me a pack of chewing tobacco."

"Like that is ever going to happen!"

"Hey, I cannot run short. I use that for a lot of different things."

"What on earth could you use that for, other than to kill your fellow flatlander?" the Kid asked, laughing.

"Well for one I give a little bit to the dogs. It helps take care of the worms," he answered, grinning at his kid brother.

"Oh my God, I have always worried that I might have worms," the Kid answered, still laughing. "But you know that stuff will kill almost anything it gets in contact with. And no wonder your dogs are half-crazy. How long have you giving them that stuff?"

"I have been giving them a little bit since they were pups. I just take a little pinch, open their mouths, and down the hatch. They don't have near the reaction that you have had. They have that cowboy working dog trust going on," Paul said, grinning.

"Yeah, I have a real understanding of that trust myself."

Laughing, the two brothers walked into the saddle shop, which smelled of oils and leather. They were saddles everywhere and just about anything else you would want as far as tack.

Walker and the Kid were laughing pretty hard, with the old cowboy filling the shop owner in on the joke. The shop owner looked at the Kid, telling him Walker had been funning with people for a long time. He also told the Kid if he swallowed the juice, it would kill any worms he might have. All three just broke up in laughter.

The Kid ordered his chaps and was almost out of money. The shop owner said it might take a while to find a cow big enough, or maybe they would have to find some other critter to make the chaps from. But he would have them done by the next time the Kid had a day off to come back to town.

"So there, you have boots and a cowboy hat, and your chaps are getting made. All you have to do now is get the cook to help you buy a fishing pole. How are you feeling? You look like you are still sweating a little," Paul said, smiling.

"I will be fine. Just keep that stuff away from me. Hey, there is June. "

"There you two are. Have you two stayed out of trouble?"

"The Kid bought cowboy boots and a hat and had to order his chaps."

"So why, Paul, do you have a big smile on your face and the Kid is a little pale and sweating?"

"June, I have just been wormed," the Kid answered, laughing.

"You have been what? Paul, what did you do to the Kid this time?"

"Hey, he just wanted to know what it was like to chew tobacco! It was all the Kid's idea I swear," Paul answered, laughing.

"Paul, that stuff will kill him! Kid, you're not going to be able to taste food for a day or two. He didn't get you to swallow the juice, did he?"

"No, are you kidding? I just spit the chaw out on the ground."

"I just knew this was a bad idea from the start. I just cannot take you two children anywhere! Now let's eat and make our way back to the ranch."

"June how about you help me buy a fishing pole?"

"I will help you buy a fishing pole on one condition."

"What is that?" "You have to start eating your veggies," she answered, smiling.

"Paul is trying to kill me with chewing tobacco, and you are worried about my health," the Kid replied, laughing.

"That's a deal breaker!"

"All right, I will eat my veggies. But you have to quit smoking cigarettes while I do. They are probably made from chewing tobacco," he said, smiling.

"I won't smoke in the cookhouse when you are eating, if you eat your veggies, deal?"

"That's a deal. Let's buy a fishing pole."

On the drive home, the Kid showed June his boots, cowboy hat, and all the things that went along with them. June thought that both items were good choices, especially the boots.

The Midwest flatlander Kid had never bought any western clothes and looked forward to riding Old Brown while looking more like a real cowboy.

Fixing Fence

The old cowboy and the Kid spent their morning fixing the barbed wire fence around the summer pasture high in the mountains. In the next couple of days, they had to get the fence in the condition to be able to hold a cow. Old Mother Nature soon was going to be running the snow out of the high mountains with her warmer temperatures. By that time, the cow and calf pairs needed to be at summer pasture, and they would use the runoff water to irrigate the ranch meadows.

After the two cowboys worked, there were only a few big places where the Kid had to come back to fix. Those places were in the low areas of the timber and mostly the same barbed wire with steel posts. But in some of the places where the lay of the land was too steep and rocky, it was jack-leg fence spliced into the barbed wire. To fix the fence in these places, the Kid had to cut small lodgepole trees down to make rails. It wouldn't take a day for an experienced hired man to do, but a flatlander from the Midwest had his work cut out for him.

The Kid was busy fixing a piece of barbed wire and saw Walker coming into view a short distance away. They met back up, and the old cowboy helped the Kid finish his splice.

"Well, how is your day going Kid?"

"Good! Paul, what did you think of the elk?"

"That bunch has been around for a while now. The herd gets a little bigger all the time. So far, even with the larger numbers, they still are not eating too much of the summer pasture that we lease from the forest service.

"The elk travel back and forth from the Big Hole valley to here. The elevation there is about sixty-three hundred feet. So it's still winter there now. It will probably be about two or three more weeks 'til the elk go back there. They like the grass there because it is just better and there are not as many people around where they go.

"If you like ranching here in this valley and want to learn more of the old ways, the Big Hole Valley is the place to live. But you better be ready for Old Mother Nature's coldest winters and mosquitoes and deer and horse flies that are big enough to ride with a saddle."

"Paul, really? The bugs cannot be that big."

"Kid, I am a telling you they are. Trust the old cowboy on this matter."

"Paul, when you are at cow camp, how much area do you cover for the summer?"

"You have to take in consideration all the things I do. I have to make sure the pairs are healthy and the bulls are doing their job, so there is some roping of calves and giving of medicine, doctoring. The bulls always seem to get a little lazy when the temperatures go up and the mosquitoes and flies come out. You have to stir them up a little, getting them interested in the cows. That is what Sam and Helper like to do, is to get the bulls on the fight.

"You also need to look out for any predators that may be around that might have mischief on their minds. So I cover a lot of ground when I am at cow camp."

"What predators are around?"

"As you have seen, it's really a little primitive here in the mountains. There are coyotes, as I am sure you already have heard and seen. There are some bears that really don't cause too many problems. Every once in a while, the forest service will transplant a problem bear here from the more-populated areas. I have always thought a problem bear is the same problem wherever it is—a problem. I believe the forest service does it to let the natives solve their problem. Besides, if the bear causes a problem here, it ends up in the stew and with the hide on the wall. We are ranchers around here, and we try to respect what the forest service does, but not at the cost of the livestock or the people who live here. Now as far as flatlanders, that's all right. We will let the bears have all of them that are around."

"I think that Old Brown would be able to outrun a bear."

"Depends on the situation. Old Brown would probably buck you off and let the bear have you."

"Paul, how about wolves?"

"What about them?"

"Are there any in the area?"

"Sure there are. Wolves are the most intelligent animal here. They don't seem to want to get to close to the livestock at this point. But the boundaries of people always seem to get further into their territory all the time. It will probably get like the bear situation with forest service."

"How do you tell a wolf from a coyote?"

"As long as I have been here in the area, I have only heard wolves and seen a couple at a distance in all that time. Like I said, they are really smart and want to stay to themselves. The size differences between a wolf and a coyote are as similar as an elk is to a deer. At a distance, you can tell the differences because one has the body language of a scavenger and the other of a predator. The coyote is on guard, looking for what another animal hasn't finished or what they can handle in there pack. A pack of wolves is the top of the food chain. Wolves' body language is confident, and they really do not care if another animal is around. They are top dog, and they know it!"

"How do you tell between a wolf and coyote when they are howling?"

"To answer that question, you just have to here a wolf howl. It is unmistakable; there is nothing like it. Here, I want to show you something up here a little ways."

Walker and the Kid rode their horses to almost the top of Lemhi pass. As they approached the ghost town, there were a few buildings off to one side. A couple of the buildings were in good shape for as old as they were. Walker thought this would be a good spot for dinner. They hobbled the horses in the grass and sat on an old porch step to eat.

"Let's see what the cook gave us for dinner. A person can get a lot of food in these old saddle bags of mine. Hey, June put our food in brown paper bags with our names on them. That's odd."

"Paul, I got a veggie sandwich and a note. I have to eat my veggies before I get anything else."

"That's funny; I got a big double slice meat loaf sandwich with catsup. Oh wait a minute, there are two for me! Hey, wait a minute, there are two pieces of chocolate cake too. You know, Kid, I cannot eat all of this food. How about you help an old cowpoke out?"

"Yeah, you two are in this together. OK, I will help an old cowpoke out. Come on, give up my food."

The two sat on a porch step in the old ghost town talking of the local history. They sat speculating on how the old ghost town had come to be where they ate lunch. What would it take for the pioneers to survive here at the place where they were eating their sandwiches? The Lewis and Clark trail was close by, and maybe this was a town that came to be from that bit of local western history.

"Paul, what do you think of the Lewis and Clark expedition since you are part native Sioux Indian and were raised on the reservation in the Dakotas? The old timers had to talk about some of their history when you were growing up."

"Well, it's like this: I think people in general have been doing what's been in their nature for a lot longer than that expedition. Some of the tribes were warring amongst themselves anyway before any whites came out west or east, for that matter. What little you and I have talked about so far in dealing with the dominant horses is the same with people. It's the same with wolves and bears. The up and coming dominant animal always wants to challenge for ownership in the pack or territory. You cannot blame an animal for what it is natural for them to do.

"But keep in mind what we have already talked about before, respect. That same respect is how you choose to win against your opponent and how you treat him or her after you have won the battle. I believe if a person thinks of how he or she would want to be treated if he or she had lost, it might be a good start for the person standing to treat the loser."

"I hear what you are telling me. How come, then, from the books I have read, the person standing isn't always the one who should be or who is the smartest? I say that because from what I have read, in some respects I really don't think much of the expedition. It really set the precedent for other whites moving west to treat all Native Americans who were here first poorly. I think it goes back to the respect issue you just mentioned. I'm not a historian, but Paul, look at how you were raised on a reservation."

"Now you're asking questions for someone a lot smarter than me. But I'll try to answer your question. Let's take the Lewis and Clark expedition. That was the beginning of the end for the tribes. There wasn't any good versus evil. There was a lot more whites than natives, with the white culture winning out in the long run. So we live by the boundaries that are set by their lifestyle. As people continue to populate the world, it is going to continue on a larger scale. The country that has the most land with the most people will have their way and promote their culture. I will be long gone by that day.

"Hey, you know, we better get going. I have to show you where the salt tubs are at and get back to the ranch so you can give old Buttercup her full body massage."

Once back at the ranch, they took care of their horses and loaded the Dodge for the next day. Tomorrow, if the Kid didn't run into any trouble, he would be easily back in time for supper. The Kid picked up the milk bucket from the cookhouse, and the old cowboy visited with the cook.

"Paul, how did your day go?"

"June, we had a good day. The Kid did fine, and I believe he will be able to handle going up there tomorrow by himself. Most of the fences he needs to fix are in the timber, and all he needs to do is cut about fifteen to twenty small lodgepole trees down, making some rails for the jack fence. The rest is no big problem if he doesn't get to it. I can finish it when I am at cow camp. Your note was a hit."

"Yeah, I thought you two would miss the cook being gone all day. Did you take him to the ghost town?"

"Yes, he likes to talk about how it was in the old times. We sat on a porch step chewing the fat about it. How did your day go?"

"Well I caught a few fish that I am frying for supper, and I found Ike's litter."

"How many does she have?"

"Five, and you are not going to say anything about me messing with litter?"

"No, I have tried my best to convince you not to do it."

"You mean after all these years you are not going to hassle me about the kittens?"

"Yep, I am a changed man. This old cowpoke has learned his lesson."

"You know, I will leave that to time. I have known you too damn long to believe that you are a changed man."

"Who is changed? The milk cow and cat still haven't changed!" the Kid said.

"Paul says he isn't going to give me grief about the cats anymore. I think that old cowboy is full of it!" June answered.

"Did Paul tell you about the elk and the ghost town?" the Kid asked.

"He hadn't said anything about the elk. How many were there?"

"Paul, what do you think, about fifty?"

"Something like that, Kid. It is the same bunch that goes between the Big Hole Valley and here. I did find a three-year-old buck that would be good for jerky."

"That's right, thanks for the jerky!"

"Kid, did you like the jerky? It is from last year's buck."

"Paul, when I am not eating the cook's food, I think I could live on jerky and spring water. I could get used to living in the mountains!"

"I am glad you said that. We should probably make some more. That buck I saw today should do the trick. But we need to let him alone for now. I like him to eat a little more of the new grass of spring to fatten him up. We will wait for the buck's coat to get good and slick. The buck has probably had a hard time of it for the winter. I like him to be fat and relaxed, maybe even sleeping when I shoot him."

"Paul, isn't that a lot of jerky? Why wait?"

"Kid, we use the back strap for steaks and some of the more choice cuts for roasts. It doesn't all go toward jerky. Why wait this long? The buck comes out of winter rundown and eats what he can find to hold him over until the winter weather is over. It is the same as those two-year-olds we have been graining. The grain, like the new grass, has more of what makes the meat better or tender to eat.

"Most people when they hunt only have time to come out to shoot something to eat. I like to pick out what I want for meat, and when it is the best time, to shoot it for taste. It makes it a chess game between me and the animal. I guess living here and being at cow camp allows me the time to pick what I want to shoot, and when it the best time, to shoot it.

"Let me say it like this. I can probably guess that you are not a hunter, so you haven't owned a rifle or handgun."

"You're right. I really haven't had the thought till now to shoot something. I just think of animals as something you watch or admire in the wilderness. The elk today were the first I have ever seen."

"I have the same appreciation for the animals. But you have to imagine that same elk herd a whole lot bigger to understand the impact it would have on the local ranchers. If we did not hunt the animals to help create the balance, that elk herd would be eating most, if not all, of the grazing that ranchers need for their stock.

"In the wilderness, all animals have what I call their individual territories that they have staked out. This elk herd stays here most of the winter because it is easier. They go back to the Big Hole Valley after the winter there is over. When it is time for the pairs to come here for summer pasture, I take the time to help the elk move back to the Big Hole Valley. I just nudge them a little in that direction to make room for the pairs. The winter is over, and that's where they want to go anyway. So the dogs and I, at a distance, move them back to where the grass is better and the pairs get to have more grass to eat. We are a large part of the food chain, whether people want to admit it or not. Everybody has to do their part to make it work!"

"OK, you two, get up to the table and eat some fresh fish I caught today. I tried a little different crumb batter today. There is also a little lemon for the fish, and we have oatmeal raisin cookies for desert."

Walker and the Kid continued to talk of hunting and the next day's work. The Kid from the beginning liked being lined out and then turned loose. He liked very much the time the old cowboy took to pass on his knowledge. He couldn't remember anybody he liked to be around more.

The next day was going to be a big test for the Midwest flatlander Kid. He was going to drive a stick shift all the way to Lemhi Pass fixing fences. The drive would take him to a place where people from where he was from came to visit for their vacation. It has Baldy, a snow-capped peak, at a distance, wild animals, a ghost town, and spring water for drinking. He loved working on the ranch!

"You should be able to get back in plenty of time for milking. I believe we have loaded all what you might need to do the job.

"While you're fixing fence, I'll move the pairs to the field where the branding is going to take place. When we start the day of branding, we put all the pairs in the corral. Then we sort out the cows and put them back in the field. That just leaves the calves in the corral. With the extra room in the corral, it gives the cowboys a horseback room to ride and rope the calves. Once the calves are branded, they go back out to their mommas in the field."

"How long does it take to brand the calves?"

"It's going to be a long day for sure. There should be quite a bit of help and great food to eat. It's a gathering of old friends and neighbors!

"Kid, it is getting late. We all better get some shut eye. Tomorrow is a long day, and we have a few more hard days ahead."

"Paul, thanks for all your help with the loading of the old Dodge and all the fun up in the mountains."

"You bet. I had a good day also, so thanks for all your good company, Kid!"

"June, how's about I take a couple of those cookies left on the plate?"

"Yeah, go ahead, and don't stay up so late reading."

"How in the world did you know I was reading?"

"Kid, June and I take a short walk sometimes at night to look at the stars. We see your light at a distance through the breaks in the chinking."

"Well I'll be! I have been reading some of my Louis L'Amour books again. The reading is quite a bit more meaningful since I have been living on the ranch. I understand more, and the words on the pages just seem to come to life now!"

"Kid, aren't you just the funny one? Take some more of the cookies and don't stay up too late."

"Thanks, June, for the cookies, and I will try to get to bed early."

The next morning started without any hitches. The Kid had a good breakfast of sourdough biscuits and gravy. The golden brown biscuits were fresh, warm, and flaky, and the gravy was made from the grease and scraps of link sausages, not brains! It's made with a little flour and fresh milk, and you stir it in the scraps till it thickens over the stove. The cook wanted to make the Kid his favorite breakfast after the night before, since he read western books and all. It had got to pulling at the cook's heartstrings.

"You are going to spoil that Kid with all that good cooking."

"Paul, he reads Louis L'Amour before he goes to bed. How can you not like the Kid?"

"I like the Kid all right. I am having as much fun as I can remember having."

"Paul, you think he will be all right in the mountains by himself?"

"That Kid is a bit smarter than you think. He seems to have done his reading on Lewis and Clark expedition, and he hasn't had any problems with any of the animals for a few weeks now."

"Yeah, he has come a long way in a short amount of time."

"Speaking of time, I had better get a horse saddled and get to moving those pairs. Let's go, dogs, we are burning daylight!"

Walker saddled his stud and rode for the branding field. Once in the branding field, all he had to do was a quick check of the fence for breaks. The lead cows would know it was almost time to go to summer pasture. They might get the idea to leave early if they found a break in the fence, so the field had to hold the pairs, at least till it was time to go on the cattle drive.

Walker and his dogs had been through quite a few brandings over the years that he had spent on this ranch. When he started working on the ranch all those years past, it was a lot more open, with not a lot of fences. A cowboy had to use his knowledge to try to get the calves branded. There was just quite a bit more for a cowboy to do.

There was always the risk of losing the cow or calf in the mountains without all the fences. Today all he had to do was open the gates between fields and trail them to where the branding was going to take place. The cows even knew the way and probably knew it was that time of year again. There was not a whole lot for an old cowboy to do.

With all the fences, the cows just had to stay paired as much as possible. He just had to let them meander slowly to the next field. It was about knowing the cows and how to get them to stay paired up. What you didn't want to happen was to get a calf and cow on opposite sides of the fence; they just looked at each other, bawling.

The old cowboy stopped on the bench above the pairs to see how they were scattered in the field in relation to the gate. The old cowboy just shrugged his shoulders, riding toward the pairs, wondering if it even mattered.

He had to get everything but the lead cows up moving toward the gate in the corner of the field first. Once all those cows were moving toward the gate, he then started the leads at the back of the herd toward the gate. Lead cows move through the rest of the pairs like they have a place to get to. There are just faster.

There were always those head-butter cows that seemed to fight the process. That's why it is called the drag. All the cows ahead of the drag had to stay paired up to prevent this. You had to go at the pace the whole herd wanted to go. If there were a lot of calves by themselves at the drag, the calves started bawling and their mommas came running back to find their calf. The whole herd forgets where they are going and turn away from the direction they are supposed to be headed! The process took some time, and a person cannot get in a hurry or the drag will be full of calves.

Walker liked working cattle by himself with his dogs. The three seemed to be somehow able to know instinctively what the others needed to get the job done. But Walker was from the old ways. He was just able to somehow make the dogs understand all of what he needed them to do.

Walker and his dogs started a few pairs in the direction of the gate. The cows that were lying down chewing their cuds got up, stretching their backs, giving the signal to their calves to come to get a little milk from their mommas. There were calves jumping, kicking, and playing flatlander football with other calves. The mommas gave a call, and the calves came a-running to find out what the momma wanted. Pretty soon the cows and calves were paired up, moving in the direction of the gate.

It looked like Walker and his dogs were going to get the pairs moved before dinner. There were a few calves that the dogs had to get after, but everything went relatively well.

Walker sat his horse at the last gate and watched to make sure that the pairs would settle in, eating a little green grass. He walked his horse to the leads, turning them back into the rest of the pairs. Then he waited again for all the pairs to have their heads down eating before he decided to leave.

"Paul, how did the morning go?"

"Those old cows know it is time to go to summer pasture. There were some of the newer calves that the dogs had to convince to leave the field. June, I have watched Sam and Helper since they were pups. It still makes a man wonder how they can be so gentle with the calves and be downright mean with bulls. Yeah, I am talking you up to the cook. She still would like it that you two would stay outside and sleep."

"You got that right about those two ornery dogs! How do you think the Kid is doing?"

"He'll get along just fine. You shouldn't worry."

"What do you have going on this afternoon?"

"Well, this won't help with your worrying, but I need to blow that beaver dam," he answered, smiling.

"You are right about that! I hate that stuff! You ought to have the boss do that."

"Old girl, the boss isn't going to want to mess with dynamite. Look what dear, sweet Buttercup did to him."

"You are just like the Kid! At your age, you still like to blow things up."

"Well a man has to have his fun sometime."

"How many shots from that old Winchester do you think you will need to get the job done?"

"Not as many as it would take for you and your little pop gun."

"Walker, I have always been able to outshoot and out-fish you!"

"Dogs, we need to finish our dinner and get to having some fun. I think the cook is worried about the Kid thinking she could ever outshoot this old cowboy."

"Yeah, old cowboy, you better hurry out the door!"

Smiling from ear to ear, the old cowboy drove his pickup through the fields with the dogs up front clearing the way, making sure the yearlings stayed in their field.

When the looking-to-have-a-little-fun old cowboy had finished putting on his waders, he paused, looking at the dynamite and wondering. He looked from the really-bigger-than-he-originally thought beaver dam to the really big firecrackers in his hands. He wondered whether he had enough to do the really serious job of blowing up sticks in the creek. Then he added one more stick to the two sticks he already had. He taped them all together with the all purpose gray tape that all natives have in their pickups for occasions just such as this.

Now with a really big smile, he waded in the creek to set the charge of dynamite that was really more than he needed. Yet again, he paused. He wanted to survey the entire pile of just little sticks looking for the right spot. More bang for special effects was his concern.

The always fun-loving old cowboy who was looking to have a little entertainment was having some last-minute thoughts of safety—really! He paused again, thinking maybe the dynamite just might be too much, so the very safety-conscious old cowboy talked it over with his army corps of engineers, Sam and Helper, that, by the way, were very carefully stepping across the dam trying to keep up with the person, their friend, who not too long ago had a stroke.

The army corps of engineers always wanted to make their fun loving; entertaining-loving old cowboy happy. They showed the demolition specialist what had to be the safest spot. They maybe even smelled the old beaver; that would be lucky!

Now the old cowboy and the two engineers were looking from the chosen spot to their old truck. The conversation was about the best way to place the charge so as to be able to shoot the really-too-big-of-a- change three sticks of dynamite away from the truck. The fun-loving old cowboy conversed with the army corps of engineers and thought maybe he should move the truck further back before he took the shot.

Once everything was just at the right angle in the right position, he waded out of the creek, almost laughing in anticipation of the gratuitous explosion of fireworks.

Back at the truck, he loaded up the army corps of engineers into the cab for what had to be the best viewing of anyone in the audience, except maybe the one pulling the trigger.

With the army corps of engineers watching, the fun-loving old cowboy used his spotting scope from under the front seat to locate the target in question. The always-concerned-about-safety, fun-loving cowboy moved the truck back a little more after looking at the two engineers sitting in the front seat.

Everything was in place as it has been before. This was not the first time this fun-loving old cowboy had played with dynamite. He had never used three sticks—there was that new aspect. Sam and Helper had been there before also and were happy the fun-loving old cowboy moved their viewing position back a little. They might even lie on the truck floorboards like before.

Now the cowboy considered a last couple of details. Where was the sun, and was there any wind? With the sun at his back, he held his trustworthy old Winchester in one hand. He stuck a finger in his mouth from the other hand and held it up, checking the direction of the wind, just in case there was any.

After he had taken his thumb and wiped away any dirt that might have been on the sight, finally the old cowboy leaned on the hood of his truck with one eye closed. As he looked down the barrel of his Winchester, holding his breath and then slowly letting it out, with his finger almost pulling the trigger, the dynamite blew!

The fun-loving old cowboy looked at his old Winchester with a look of disbelief. He hadn't pulled the trigger! He looked at his army corps of engineers sitting in the front seat for their help in determining what possibly could have happened. Then he heard the most dreadful sound of laughing from a distance—the cook!

Shaking his head, the very disappointed old cowboy, with slumped shoulders and a hint of a smile on his face, drove his truck to check on the pairs just one more time on his way back to the ranch.

He drove his truck around the perimeter of the fence, checking all the animals. Everything looked fine. The calves were all playing or sucking their moms' bag for milk. There were cows lying down chewing their cuds. That's always a good sign. Walker felt good that it would be all right to leave them and go back to the ranch disgraced as a fun-loving old cowboy.

As he entered the hideout of the would-be long-distance assassin, he paused in the mudroom. It was almost reminiscent of when the Kid had to take his lumps from his head-butting football yellow flag controversy. As the fun-loving old cowboy approached the line of demarcation, he took the same deep breath as the Kid and walked in.

There, smiling from ear to ear, was the would-be assassin. They stood looking at each other eye to eye. The fun-loving old cowboy was familiar with the look from all the other times his beloved, the would-be assassin, had taken the entertainment from his day.

"What do you think. Paul? Pretty good shooting for a cook with her pea shooter."

"How long were you there?"

"I was able to witness most of your setup while I waited to take my shot."

"You're kind of sassy today. You have never been able to outshoot this old cowboy. That was just a lucky shot! I give you the fishing. But you cannot outshoot my old Winchester. You don't even clean yours. How do you expect it to shoot straight?"

"I bet I can shoot one of those ornery dogs of yours at couple hundred yards!"

"My, June, you are sassy today! You better leave my dogs out of this conversation. They don't eat as much as the Kid."

"Where is he anyway? He should have been here by supper."

"June, the Kid is just fine. He is off by himself in the mountains driving the old Dodge he likes so well! But I'll help out the flatlander and do his milking for him."

"You sure old Buttercup will let you after the Kid has worked his magic on her?"

"My you are sassy. I will do just fine. I'll take my Winchester just in case. I should be able to get close enough to hit the cow in one shot."

"Make sure you get her in the barn first before you take the shot."

"Old girl, you need to give me the milk bucket so I can stop this abuse. Come on, dogs, you better come and help me to milk the old cow. I might need the protection, and it might be safer for you if you do."

Walker and his dogs were having a good day. Since his stroke, he was just beginning to feel like his old self. The dogs liked having Walker back up to speed. They liked the old cowboy so much that the dogs could not help but nip at his pant leg bottoms as they all walked to the barn.

"Come on in here, you old milk cow. Remember me? I am the old cowboy that got you started. The Kid isn't back yet, so I have to help out and do the milking.

"Yeah, you two can come in and I'll shut the stall gate. Where is that old cat? Might as well let her in here with the rest of the animals so we can make it all warm and cozy.

"Buttercup, the Kid talks up a storm about how good you are now. I think it is how this old cowboy got you started. You know, Buttercup, I have been doing this all my life. Even though I am from the Dakotas, I consider myself to be a native. I worked with the old man when he was here. So I am taking credit for how good you are! Hey, I can hear the cat coming."

The scene was set. Walker was milking dear, sweet Buttercup at about half a milk bucket. The dogs were lying quietly in the corner of the stall by the gate.

The dogs were looking forward to getting some milk. It had been a while. Since the Kid started doing the milking, the dogs had not gotten their portion and were watching every drop go in the milk bucket.

Ike showed up late because she had been taking care of her litter and was also preoccupied with getting her share of milk. Ike heard the commotion and ran as fast as she could down the hallway of the barn. At a full-out sprint, she scaled the stall gate to the milking stall, landing in the middle of the dogs. Oh, that was bad!

What happened next is what anybody would expect to have happened. Dear, sweet Buttercup was so upset that she not only kicked at all the other animals she nailed her mentor in the leg and drilled the milk bucket her second try! The scene looked like something out of the rodeo.

"Paul, what in the heck happened to you? Oh my God! Look at the milk bucket; and you're limping!"

"I'll be fine."

"Did that dear, sweet old Buttercup nail you?"

"Yeah, that's what a man wants to hear from his woman after he has taken his life in his own hands trying to milk that old milk cow."

"You better let the Kid milk that old cow. He seems to have her figured out."

"I got her figured out! I just let my guard down is all."

Walker told his story to the cook and was beginning to see the humor of what had just happened.

"I better go put a change of clothes on before the Kid gets back. Where is he, by the way? He should have been here a long time ago!"

"Paul, I can start to see his truck lights now coming down the road from out the window."

"I had better limp into the bedroom and change before he gets here. You are going to behave yourself and let me tell the Kid what happened."

The lights from the old Dodge turned into the main ranch. The Kid stepped out, still laughing from all the fun fixing fence high in the mountains of Montana.

The Kid walked in and sat in his chair, smiling. The dogs somehow seemed different, and the cook had a great big smile on her face.

"Well, you made it back in one piece."

"June, I did, but have I got a story to tell! Where is Paul?"

"Kid, Paul wasn't as lucky as you were."

"Old girl, you better let me tell my story!"

"Paul, what in the heck happened to your leg?"

"That damn milk cow of yours kicks pretty fast! How did your day go?"

"It went all right. First tell me what happened to you."

"The cook here got me all fired up. Since you left this morning, she has been as ornery as that old cow of yours. I moved the pairs just fine in the morning.

"This is where my train comes off the track. I should have taken some jerky with me and not come to eat dinner. I have been reading stock animals my whole life so I can stay out of trouble. I knew this morning at breakfast that the cook was on the fight!"

"Wait a minute, you are calling me a stock animal?"

"Old girl, let me tell my story! See, Kid, what I have been going through while you were gone. Anyway, after dinner I needed to blow the beaver dam."

"Paul, I wanted to help with that!"

"Kid, help me out here and just listen to my story! The dogs and I got three sticks of dynamite from the storage shed. When we got to the beaver dam, we set the charges of dynamite. I took my Winchester that was handed down to me from my relatives. You know that old Winchester shot at Yellow Hair at his pitiful last stand. It is a family treasure!"

"Paul, you are not that old to have fought at Custer's last stand!"

"Kid, don't encourage him to go on and tell this fairy tale of his."

"No, Kid, my relatives! Now listen to the story! I had to take my old Winchester and shoot the dynamite. I took close aim, took a breath, let the breath out slowly, and squeezed the trigger. I hit the dynamite in one shot."

"The heck! I shot the dynamite from atop on the sage brush bench!"

"Who is telling the story anyhow? So I came back to the cookhouse and told the cook it took me three shots, just to make her feel better. Why, you ask? The cook has said for years that she can outshoot this old cowboy. I have been letting her believe that for years!"

"What does this have to do with you limping? And oh, look at the smashed milk bucket."

"Kid, I am getting to that. Since you were not back yet, I thought I would help out and do your milking. So I am limping because you trained that dear, sweet Buttercup all wrong." "Buttercup kicked you! Oh that's funny!"

"Oh, by the way, the cook wants to take shots at good old Sam and his wonderful daughter. I felt bad for the dogs hearing such awful things coming from the cook, their adopted mother. I decided to let them into the milking stall so they could have some fresh milk. I usually make them stay out in the barn hallway. But like I said, I felt bad for them. Everything was going fine when …

"Where is Ike?" "

That is what caused the wreck. Ike hadn't showed up when we started to do the milking. The dogs were lying in the corner of the stall next to the gate."

"Oh my God, Ike always just jumps that gate!"

"Yep, you know that old cat. She must have been training all this time to be able to jump that gate. When she did jump that gate, she landed in the middle of the dogs. Everything had to be in the right spot to make it all happen at once!"

"Is Ike all right?"

"June, the Kid is asking if the cat is all right. I am sitting here with a bum leg and he is worried about the cat! Yeah, Kid, she is fine. So that dear, sweet Buttercup of yours kicked me in the leg, smashing the milk bucket in the process. I could not tell you how she was able to kick me, the bucket, and have all the other animals scattering for cover, but they all ran out of there like ants leaving an ant hill!"

"Were you able to finish milking?

Yes, the old cow had her fun, and I wondered what the Kid would do now. I gave her some more oats."

"Driving home I thought I had excitement during the day."

"Kid, take your time and go ahead tell your story. But tell the real story, not some fable as this old cowboy of mine just did."

"Well, it was like this. After leaving the main ranch, the drive was good. The sun started coming up over the mountains and made everything glow in reds and yellows. The old Dodge and I are beginning to be old friends, so there were no problems there. I saw some animals along the way, some antelope down low in the fields. There were also some mule deer in some trees as I got higher in the mountains.

"After I arrived at summer pasture, I drove to the first high ridge I could find. I sat in the old Dodge eating jerky waiting to see what I could see. June, that was a terrific breakfast of biscuits and gravy this morning, by the way."

"Thanks, Kid, but go on with your story."

"As I ate my jerky and looked around, there was a herd of elk about two hundred yards away warming themselves on a east facing ridge. I believe they were the same elk herd Paul and I saw yesterday. I watched them a while and started for the timber where the fence needed fixing. You know I put that old Dodge in second low like the old John Deere and let it go on its own. I just looked around on the way to the fence while chewing on a piece of jerky!

"Once at the fence, I knocked all the broken rails off the jack fence. Then I cut enough small lodgepole trees down to make enough replacement rails and cut them to length, nailing them on the fence. By that time, the sun was high in the horizon and it was time to eat. I cleaned up all the trimmings from the trees, spreading them out like no one had been there. The old broken rails I put in between the jacks, maybe for someone to use as firewood sometime. I felt good that I had done all that without a hitch. The fence I thought looked all right, and I let the old Dodge take me to another ridge, where I sat in the truck eating my dinner.

"The elk had moved a little but really did not mind that I was there at all. After I finished eating, I thought I would go do that little bit of fence that Paul showed me on the way out. I parked the truck next to the road, taking what I needed to walk the fence. I estimated that the fence was about a mile long. I thought it would be just as easy to walk as drive the ridge the whole way, stopping and starting all the time on the road. It took me a couple hours, maybe a little more, to walk and fix that section of fence."

"Well, Kid, sounds like you had a good day."

"But Paul, the story isn't over. When I finished with the fence, all I had to do was get back to the truck! I walked and walked, but I could not for the love of God find it. I had parked the truck off the side of the road next to the fence that I was fixing. It was an easy find! I kept walking, and the truck never showed up! I thought I had lost the old Dodge truck!"

"Kid, you lost the old Dodge flatbed truck? How in the heck did you get home?"

"June, listen to the rest of my story. The only thing I could think of at the time was Paul and the time not too long ago that I tried to butt heads with a yearling. Well, if I wanted Paul to forget that, I just added one more thing to the list for him to try to forget!"

"Yeah, that's going to take me some time to let that settle."

"So I started laughing and put my tools down next to the side of the road, where for sure I would not lose them. I even flagged the fence with my handkerchief from my back pocket. There was no way I could lose the tools.

"So with a sense of urgency, I started retracing my steps, remembering what Paul had told me, that if ever I mistreated the old Dodge, she would leave me stranded. Paul, I was good to the old truck!

"Mind you, I parked that old Dodge next to the fence off the road. I was thinking I must have walked right past it. I had to. That was the only explanation I could come up with."

"Kid how in the world could you walk past the old Dodge?"

"June, that was the only thing I thought I could have done, so I walked and walked for a lot more than a couple miles. I was laughing so hard because I could not find the old Dodge. I am telling you two, it was gone!

"Now the only thing I could think of was, 'Flatlander, you are in a world of Buttercup manure now!' I was just glad I still had a little bit of jerky left and that I knew where there was fresh water, 'cause I was spending the night. I could not walk home. It's too far."

"Kid, how did you get home?"

"Paul, it happened like this. I thought that I should sit on the fence and see if I could figure a way to get back to the ranch. Heck, if I were anywhere else, civilization, for instance, I would have thumbed my way back. I just sat and shook my head in disbelief. I thought for sure I had lost the old, rusted-out, cracked windshield, no brakes, which would be nice to have for stopping, Dodge covered in gray tape and baler twine, and it was going to come out of my paycheck if I ever made it back to civilization!

"Then I thought even though the old Dodge is real tough shape, my paychecks aren't that big, and I would be paying for it for months, maybe even years! I couldn't stop laughing now! I had tears running down my face, and those tears were not tears of joy, because now it was getting late and the sun I watched come up was setting. It was starting to get colder, and I was thankful my new broke-in cowboy boots are dry.

"The only thing now I could think of was I should have read something about this in one of my western books that I have, but I don't think there were any Sacketts who lost or misplaced the ranch pickup. I really didn't know what to do."

"Come on. Kid, you are killing us both. You got to tell us how you got back!"

"I sat on the fence, shaking my head. I then looked up at Lemhi Pass—you know, the same pass the Lewis and Clark expedition traveled over never losing anything! I don't know why I looked up there. But there sat the old Dodge. Heck, I don't even know how far away it was. I was so relieved that there the old Dodge was. But how in the heck did it get up there? I parked it way down here, not up there on the pass!"

"Kid, listen to me. Sometimes when you are in the mountains, things just get turned around. You shouldn't think a thing about it."

"Paul, but the old Dodge started moving down off the pass in my direction! The only thing I could think of was someone's trying to steal the old piece of crap Dodge covered in gray tape and baler twine, and they are coming my way! You two know me, know how big I am, and that I have not shaved or gotten a haircut for the time I have been on the ranch. So I was looking pretty scary, to say the least. I ran back to where the tools were. Yeah, I found the tools easy enough, thank God!

"I picked up the fence stretchers and pliers, waiting in the middle of the road! The truck kept getting closer and closer. The only thing I could think of was, 'They are not getting past me! I am not walking back, and I am not going to pay for that old piece of crap of a Dodge!'"

"Kid, I don't think I can take anymore. Please tell us what happened!"

"June, let the Kid tell his story."

"Well, the old Dodge stopped right in front of me standing in the middle of the road! There was a boy and middle-aged man in the cab. The man stuck his head out the driver's door missing window and said that I looked really upset and that he had a perfectly good explanation, but that I had to put the tools down before he would come out.

"Only thing I could think of was, 'That ain't going to help you! I am as big as a hotcake-eating moose now that I have been eating June's cooking!' So I laid the tools down, and the man got out of the pickup, with the boy hiding behind him."

"Yeah, Kid, you really like my sourdough hotcakes."

"June, your hotcakes are the best! The story goes like this. There were four of them, two adults and two sons, in their little Lewis and Clark expedition. They are geologists working in the field and decided to take their sons on the trip. They were in the mountains surveying and had rented a utility vehicle with four-wheel drive to use. They had driven the vehicle to where they shouldn't have, and it quit on them.

"They tried to get it started, and like a lot of us, they really don't know a lot about how to get trucks started once they quit. So they walked all the way back to the top of the pass and looked both ways. The fathers sent their young sons in each direction looking for help. The son that came my way found the old Dodge and looked around for someone that it belonged to. I, of course, was fixing fence the other way. He just got in the old Dodge, driving back to the fathers at the top of the pass!

"So let me say this now. The boy could have been maybe twelve years old. He was just barely able to see over the dash. The dad said he was so proud of his son that he had made it all the way to the pass with that old beater truck. You see, the twelve-year-old boy has never driven a clutch before. He drove all the way up to the pass without once popping the clutch and stalling the old Dodge truck, all the while trying to look over the dash. I thought to myself, 'A twelve-year-old drove that old truck better than I did!' I told the father it isn't nice to brag about his son!"

"Kid, but what took you so long?"

"June, this is what took so long. They wanted me to drive them over the pass into Idaho to find a phone to use to call someone to come and get them. So we all loaded up in the old Dodge. I had the fathers sit in the back with the fencing supplies and the youngsters up front in the cab."

"Paul, what is the likelihood of me not popping that clutch?"

"Kid, you didn't."

"I sat behind the steering wheel and looked at the shifter knob, giving the twelve-year-old boy a look of, 'Wow you did this all by yourself!' He looked at me like most natives, no big deal!"

"Kid, did you pop the clutch?"

"Yep, I did and almost dumped the fathers out on the ground from the back of the truck! I looked over at the smiling youngsters growling and drove them to Tendoy, Idaho. As you both know, that is just at the bottom of the road over the pass. I made sure that someone was coming and started my way back. That is why I am late."

The three friends sat visiting about their day till late. They retold different parts of the stories over just to hear them again. The laughter could be heard from outside the cookhouse and had the animals' ears twitching to hear all the commotion at the late hour. They ate their supper, visited, and finally had enough. They said their good nights, hoping the next day would bring the same amount of excitement.

The Kid's First Branding

Old Mother Nature's sun was just starting to come up over the snow-covered peaks with the most beautiful colors of the West. She was almost offering an apology for all her less-than-good behavior during the recent winter past—almost! After the long, hard winter of feeding and calving, the day of branding arrived, a celebration of sorts for the natives. Walker and the Kid had already saddled their horses, riding toward the pairs, wanting to get the pairs corralled early to start the process of separating them from each other. The day would be long, and the work would be hard till the branding was done.

At the start of the day, the old cowboy gave the Kid his first rope to use. He thought the Kid might like to try roping a calf or two. Walker showed the Kid how you were supposed to hold the rope in your right hand while keeping your reins in his other hand from the hackamore.

The Kid just for looks went right to slapping the rope on his right leg, riding for the pairs, and wished he had the time off to go to town and pick up his new chaps. Then he would really look the part of a cowboy at the branding!

Walker and the Kid started walking their horses around the outside of the pairs that were still lying down, trying to shake off the night's chill. They made an easy loop to get them all up, letting the calves get a little milk from their mommas to start their day.

Walker reminded the Kid to try not to break the pairs up. There was no use in getting excited. It hadn't been but a short time, and the two cowboys had the pairs drifting in the direction of the corral. The old cows just seemed to know that branding was the next step to go to summer pasture.

Working cattle for the first time and riding a horse was fast becoming a way of life for the Kid. Not only had he dreamed about it, but now he had also been living! These days on the ranch, he was experiencing were what dreams were worth working for, or in his case, taking a chance and calling a phone number. There was an absolute chance, if he had not called the number or the boss hadn't answered the phone, which wasn't out of the realm of possibilities, that his dream would not have happened. All the details that happened by chance that got him to where he was at were extraordinary, to say the least. The Kid was not anybody special and did not even deserve it more than another. He was just the lucky one to be at the right place at the right time. It was almost like someone had the thought that it was time to make some young man happy.

"Kid, we got them in. Let's close the gates and let them settle till the rest of the help shows up. What do you think of your rope?"

"The rope gives me something to do with my right hand."

"Here, let me show you how to throw a loop."

The old cowboy walked his horse about ten feet from the corral fence. He uncurled a loop, and with one easy motion, he dropped it over the top of a corral post. The Kid couldn't believe how quickly and smoothly Walker threw the loop.

"Kid, there is a little bit of information you should know before you throw your first loop. You have to remember to keep your thumb up when you dally around the horn of your saddle. If you do not and your thumb is down, chances are the thumb will be gone! It gets caught between the rope and the horn. When the calf feels the pressure of the rope, it is going to pull hard. If your thumb is in the way, it is a goner! Just keep that in mind. Now go ahead throw a loop."

The Kid backed Old Brown up a few feet, trying to duplicate how Walker threw his loop, and quickly found out that it wasn't as easy as the old cowboy had made it look. He discovered that there is a lot going on when you are throwing a loop from a horse. He continued to try a few more times.

By this time, the other folks started to show up. There were trucks and trailers of all different shapes and sizes. Cowboys, cowgirls, and cow kids started to unload their horses for the branding, with all kinds of horses, saddles, and tack. Every person, young and old, had their own system of western clothes that made them look different from the others.

The Kid was beginning to get a little nervous from all the new folks showing up. Other than in town, this was really more people he had seen at one time in quite a while. He quickly thumb-rolled his rope in tight coils like the old cowboy had shown him, hanging it back on the saddle. Then he walked Old Brown a short distance away to watch as the people unloaded all their gear and horses. The Midwest flatlander was off to himself as the natives shook hands and all the dogs growled at each other.

Then, to add to his uneasiness, an older woman was walking in his direction like she had a purpose in mind. The woman looked to be around eighty years of age. She wore a cowboy hat that looked the same age, with sweet stains and its bent-up brim showing her wrinkled, sun-tanned face. She had on worn chaps, a purple western shirt with snaps up the front, and a gray silk bandana, with spurs making that sound that spurs make, jingling! She carried a pair of new chaps for the Kid from the Midwest.

"Since you are the only one here I don't know, these must be yours! I was in town at the saddle shop to buy some new tack, and he said to give these to you. I wondered what in the world could wear chaps this big. I guess I now know!"

The Kid stepped down off Old Brown to shake hands, thanking her for taking all the trouble while trying on his new chaps. The chaps were double stitched and full length, with a heavy duty zipper down the back. The chaps were the color of leather—brown with a light red tint. Those colors would change a little once the Kid oiled the chaps with neat's foot.

The woman looked on in appreciation that the chaps looked like they would do their job. The chaps looked a lot like Walker's, just not worn around the bottoms; Sam and Helper would maybe take care of that!

"Now that I have met you, Flatlander, I just have one question. Did you really lose that old Dodge truck, and as big as you are, did that yearling survive you butting it in the head?"

"Then you already know I am from the Midwest, a flatlander. By the way, that's two questions!"

"Well, you better give me your arm and walk me to the rest of the folks. Hey, don't let Paul give you any bull about being from the Midwest. I have known that kid since he was your age, and he is from the Dakotas. So that makes him the same as you, a flatlander. But all our relatives are all from somewhere else that lives here in the West. Maybe you are the first of yours to get started here. Now come and meet some of the folks. Just do me this one favor."

"Sure, what is the favor?"

"I am an old lady, and I can't fight as well as I used to. When it is time, let me go through the dinner line before you."

"Oh, you're a riot! Did Paul tell you to say that?"

The old native and the flatlander walked over to what was becoming a pretty big crowd of people. The old woman introduced the Kid as the second flatlander in the valley, all the while smiling at Walker. Everyone wanted to hear the Kid's story of head butting and if he really lost the old Dodge pickup.

The Kid just lost his nervousness and had never felt so quickly at ease with new people. Everyone listened to his short versions of what happened. By the time he finished, they all were laughing with the Kid.

As they all started walking to their horses, the old woman asked Walker why he was limping so badly. Everybody just broke out laughing all over again. Smiling, the fun-loving old cowboy just shook his head, looking in the direction of the cook while stepping into the stirrups.

Everybody worked at separating the cows from the calves as if they had been doing it together their whole lives, which they had. There were folks on horses roping and others getting ready to wrestle the calves.

After a calf is roped, one person takes the calf by the front legs and another takes the back legs, giving the rope back to the roper. They sit on the ground, holding the calf's legs so that the other folks can do their respective jobs. The flatlander Kid, of course, was learning to hold the calves with the rest of the Kids.

The calf gets branded, ear tagged, dehorned, a growth enhancer, gets the tip of the left ear sliced off for identification, gets the wattle cut for identification, penicillin for infection, a ladle full of some liquid to keep the flies away that someone pours down the middle of the calves' back, and finally castrated if a bull calf! The Kid was in total disbelief that all that gets done to a calf that is only on average a few months old. What a way to start the day if you are a calf!

The first time the branding iron made a brand on a calf, he was helping to hold and had his first smell of burnt hair. The smoke just engulfed his face, with his eyes and nose burning from the smoke. The smell was awful, absolutely the worst he had ever smelled. The old woman was branding the calf he is holding.

"Yeah, Kid, I have been doing this my whole life and I am telling you, I have never gotten used to the smell."

The morning went on without a hitch. The sound of the pairs was almost deafening from all the calves and cows bawling! The branded calves stood with their tails swinging back and forth to somehow reach the hip that was branded! Some calves just stood quivering from all the things that had been done to them, and the mommas stood around the outside of the corral bawling at the scene!

It had already been a few hours since the folks started, and they had branded quite a few calves. Everybody, including the Kids of all ages, was working together, developing a steady pace. If a wrestler got tired, he or she switched with someone doing something else. Nobody is just doing one thing.

By this time, the Kid had already learned to wrestle calves, ear tag, dehorn, vaccinate, slice an ear, and pour that ladle full of liquid down the calves' backs. All he had to do now was brand, castrate, and rope a calf to be able to do all of what needs to get done at a branding.

The Midwest flatlander Kid has been kicked, shit on, and run over by the calves. He couldn't believe that a little calf could be so strong and amazingly quick. A little calf that did not reach up to his waist could be stronger than himself! Maybe it was the sight of the previous calf and all that happened to it that made the little feller struggle so hard. The Kid thought that would do it for him. But there were techniques to learn if the flatlander Kid was to watch one of the other kids.

When you first get the calf from the roper, hold the calf's legs straight up in the air. The calf is on its back helpless, and both wrestlers can get a solid hold on the legs that they are responsible for. The calf can do nothing put kick at the air!

When a wrestler is on the ground holding the back legs, take one of your feet covering the calf's butt! The first thing that happens to a calf is that it loses all that is inside from all the excitement—a mighty bowel movement! It was one even Buttercup would appreciate! If a wrestler isn't prepared, your boots get covered, maybe more! The Kid had experienced all those different techniques and results. It was all about watching and learning from what other folks did.

It was a busy morning, and it was time for dinner. The Kid was taking the time to check himself over. His new hat looked like it had been through years of ranching, with sweat working its way through the band. His creek-water-broke-in boots were comfortable but unrecognizable from all the times he forgot to cover the hind end of a calf. He had long since taken his chaps off from the hard work! The Midwest flatlander Kid looked at himself, smiling, and felt he had a good morning because he looked like everybody else.

The food was set up on a few truck tailgates that were backed up together in a line. The food looked like what you would expect. All kind of sandwiches, potato and macaroni salads, potato chips, pies, cakes, cookies, with all the pop and lemonade you could drink! The Kid was hungry and got in line after the older woman.

"Now, Kid, make sure you get some oysters! You probably haven't eaten anything like them being you are from the Midwest. We do not want anything to go to waste, so if you don't get to finish all of the goodies, this will all be here for supper, so fill up your plate!"

The Kid started to pile up his plate and caught Walker smiling at him, and he smiled back, continuing down the line of people. The Hotcake Kid put a big homemade bun with shredded roast beef on his plate, adding a couple of thin slices of tomato, a little shredded lettuce, and a mixture of catsup and mayo. Oh, that sounds good!

There was potato salad; he got a couple of spoonful's of that also. Then he came to what looked like something round stuffed with meat that looked grilled. Thinking to himself, This is what she wanted me to try, he put a few of them on his plate. He had more than enough food and walked over to the fun-loving old cowboy with his plate and lemonade.

"Hey, Kid, looks like you got enough to eat! How is your first branding going?"

"Paul, those little calves go through a lot!"

"Yeah, I wish that it could be different. Once we are done here today, we go help the other folks brand and let the little buggers mother up for a couple of days. That helps."

The Kid was eating his food and noticed folks watching him a little. Maybe they had never seen anyone his size eat so much.

"Paul, what is the wattle for?"

"Kid, the little bit of skin that is cut away from the neck hangs to help identify the calf. Folks brand in different places, and the wattle, cut ear, and ear tag help in combination with the brand for identification. Most ranchers now really have no need to cut an ear or use a wattle for identification. We do it more out of tradition than anything else."

"Why do we dehorn the calves?"

"It helps to protect us and the other animals from the horns. When I was working cattle way back when, there was always somebody getting gored or someone lost a dog. It also helps to get the big bulls through the shoot when we work them there. It is just an easy thing to do right now to make things a lot safer down the road."

"I watched the folks castrate the bull calves, and I have to tell you, it kind of hit home!"

"Yeah, when you get back to civilization and hitched back up to the blond swimmer, then it will really hit home. You really don't want to show your lady friend how to do it. I made that mistake with the cook."

"Yeah, OK, I noticed folks did the castration differently."

"I think the best way is to slice the scrotum down the middle. Then a person needs to reach in with one of his hands pulling the nuts out between the two fingers. You now have to pull, almost tearing the balls off from the connecting tissue. Then I take my sharp pocket knife and run its edge back and forth till the strings tear loose, and then a little disinfectant in and around the scrotum."

"Paul, why is most everybody looking our way?"

"You really don't want me to say!"

"OK, Paul, what have you done to me now?"

"Kid, the folks probably haven't seen a kid your size eat before. Maybe they're just a little curious how you liked all the food."

"Well I am going to get some dessert. Do you want anything?"

"No, I think eating all those Rocky Mountain oysters filled me up. I think I will wait for supper to eat some pie."

"Wait a minute, those were what the older woman wanted me to try. I don't think I remember how they tasted. What were those things anyway?"

"Those little round things that look like calf nuts?"

The Kid looked at the cowboy who was always looking to have a little fun, wondering if this was just another joke. But he just had that look of,

"That's what you ate!"

"Paul, you're telling me I just ate testicles!"

"Kid, in some areas of the world they are a delicacy!"

The Kid just looked at his empty plate where the delicacy had been. But like the other internal organs and chewing tobacco, he was having a little concern. The only thought that came to mind was how the fun-loving old cowboy had just described, in detail, how he would castrate a bull calf! The Kid could only start laughing and thought he would wait on the peach cobbler.

Everybody had been watching the scene unfold. They all knew the Kid had butchered and his friends had teased him about the brains, heart, and tongue. They just wanted to see his reaction to eating fresh Rocky Mountain Oysters for the first time.

"Kid, let me see those new chaps. You have spent the morning on the ground. Let's get you roping a little."

The two cowboys walked to where the horses were tied up with the always-looking-for-fun old cowboy still funning with the Kid about how is best to castrate a bull calf and going into great detail to make the Kid just a little more queasy! The old cowboy even told the Kid that there is a festival up in northern Montana where the main course is testicles of all types! The festival is of course called Montana Testicle Festival; it's all you can eat!

The Kid smiled broadly, shaking his head, showing the old cowboy his new chaps. He had the saddle shop double the leather at the bottoms of the legs just in case he sometime would have a dog that liked to chew on his chaps!

The Kid now was ready to ride Old Brown, having yet another piece of his cowboy wardrobe, and thought how good all the folks' efforts were today to make sure he had the chaps on the first day he branded. Even though he did not have much experience as a cowboy, he would at least look the part and feel better that he looked like anybody else, maybe.

The two cowboys walked their horses to water and tightened the cinches. Walker wanted to give the Kid some instruction on how to rope a calf. The Kid had tried a few times throwing a loop over the top of a corral post without any success. But he had learned working on the ranch you just jumped in and tried to do it. Roping is no different.

The old cowboy roped a few calves and said the Kid should go try. Walker cut out a calf from the rest so that it would be a little easier. The Kid caught the calf by one of the back legs. Then, like the old cowboy had told him, dallied thumb up, dragging the calf to the wrestlers. He thumb-rolled his rope and went back for another with a loop ready.

"Well, you picked that up pretty quick."

"It must have been all the testicles I ate!"

The Kid roped with Walker for most of the afternoon. The day was getting long, and he still had to learn to brand and yes, castrate a bull calf.

The Kid stepped down off Old Brown and loosened the cinch, rubbing the old war pony's neck and thanking him for the good day. There were some problems after he had roped his first calf, but he felt that the afternoon had gone well. Old Brown should get a lot of the credit!

He walked over to the folks who were branding, starting his lesson. Once the wrestlers were set, he had to brush any dirt off the hide and then place the hot branding iron on the hide just hard enough to brand the hide but not too hard to burn through the hide into the muscle. He had to hold the branding iron solid against the hide and not twist the iron.

"Hey, Kid, how's your day going?"

"June, I think I am going to make it."

"When you are done there, I'll show you how to castrate a bull calf."

The Kid just smiled to himself, thinking of what Paul had told him earlier.

"I am not sure that is something I want to learn how to do."

"You cannot be squeamish about it."

"I don't think I am squeamish. Paul says that maybe it's something I leave to the rest of the folks."

"Why would Paul say that? He taught me to do it a long time ago. I don't really think anything about it now!"

"I think that is Paul's point. He says that when I catch up with Nan, that castration may not be something I should consider her to know!"

They both laughed, with the Kid starting to castrate his first bull calf, the last thing he needed to learn at the branding.

The branding crew finished their day by eating all the good leftovers and telling old stories about each other of days gone past, just to entertain the Midwest flatlander Kid!

After all the good conversation was finished, everyone loaded up their trucks and trailers, making their way home. Sam and Helper were wandering around the branding corral for any scraps that were left. The only thing left to do was for Walker and the Kid to make sure that all the pairs had survived the day healthy. Then the next step was to trail the pairs to the summer pasture.

Cattle Drive

After Old Mother Nature's long winter, the day had finally come for the old cowboy to trail the pairs to summer pasture. After all the time recovering from his stroke, he was just now beginning to feel like his old self. Even as tough as he was, it still takes time to get over a stroke from more than a year ago.

During the last part of his time recuperating, the boss hired the Midwest flatlander kid to help out with the day-to-day chores. The old cowboy thought the Kid had worked out just fine, if for no other reason the Kid was a lot of fun to be around.

The fun-loving old cowboy enjoyed teasing the flatlander Kid. He just seemed to have a genuinely good-natured way about himself. The flatlander Kid's hard work had helped Walker get back to where he liked to be, in the mountains with his dogs, Sam and Helper. Now he could ride his horses and see what was the same and what had changed! The old cowboy only had to trail the pairs to summer pasture and then gather up his belongings to make it to his cow camp high in the mountains of Montana for the summer.

But as it happens, Old Mother Nature did not seem to want to cooperate. She had waited, trying to be benevolent in her desires, and had even let them brand her little calves. She thought maybe she should give them a break from all her bad-weather antics, but that was boring.

Like all the previous generations, Old Mother Nature wanted to make it hard on all the cowboys driving cattle to summer pasture, especially the Kid. She knew the Kid had been on the ranch long enough to know that her weather was just something that you had to accept. But Old Mother Nature had her eye on the Kid and wanted to see the Midwest flatlander struggle. She thought maybe she would get lucky and break him, sending back to the city. So now she wanted to have some fun and enjoy her spring, when any and everything can happen.

It was an early morning, and the two cowboys were talking of the day's work ahead, wearing their rain slickers and riding to the branding field.

The Kid was listening to Walker tell him how the day was going to work. There were gates to open and close. Even though they had fixed the fence in the summer pasture, that didn't necessarily mean the fences along the way were in good shape. A cowboy always has to keep his eyes open for trouble along the way.

Walker suggested that the Kid stay on the drag, watching the other cowboys to see how it all worked. Then if he felt like he could do something else, he should trade with one of the other cowboys. But once the pairs started, there was no coming back, no matter how bad the weather was to get. You just had to cowboy up and finish what you started.

Everybody started to show up, wearing yellow rain slickers and rubber overshoes on their cowboy boots from the already darkening clouds looming in the morning sky! Their yellow rain slickers draped over the back of the saddle and then down over their legs, with snaps up the front. Those two pieces of clothing alone would make the day easier. Just about anything else could get wet and a cowboy could make it.

The pairs were starting to get up, stretching from the restful night's sleep. The calves were sucking their mommas, playing together like something was going to happen. It was in the air. All the animals seemed to feel the weather change right before it showed up. Even in calving, if the weather changed, you could bet there would be some new calves on the ground. You could watch horses in a field jumping and kicking right before a change in weather.

Riders and their dogs were slowly starting to push the pairs in the direction of the gate, showing the opening to the pairs closest. Once the first few pairs would go through the gate, the rest would follow like water through a head gate. All that had to happen now was that the other cows had to notice the other pairs going through the double jack-leg gate.

As he worked the drag, the Kid started slapping his rope on his thigh, enjoying the sound of cattle bawling. The Midwest flatlander Kid cowboy was on his first cattle drive. He was going to enjoy himself despite the weather that was surely on its way.

The herd was spread out where a person could start to see the individual pairs. It was remarkable to the Kid how the calf resembled its mom. A lot of the pairs even had the same pattern of colors. He could see personalities match also. If a mom was a little trouble, the calf was probably going to show the same inclination.

Even Old Brown knew what was going on. The Kid gave the old horse his head, and Old Brown would do the deciding on what needed to be worked back in the herd. The Kid would try to go here and Brown would take him somewhere else. Maybe he would just watch the old war pony, seeing if he made the same choices.

Walker was hazing the herd along the west side, checking fences and gates as he rode. He had few problems so far and only asked his dogs a couple times to do their jobs. The weather looked a little better, and for that he was thankful, hoping the Kid would have a good day on his first cattle drive.

The cattle were bawling, with the cowboys slapping their ropes against their chaps riding their horses, keeping the cattle together and going in the right direction. It was a scene that made Walker remember old times when he did the trailing in the open country, when it was just the old man, him, and the dogs trailing a herd of about six hundred to the stock yards in Hamilton. Now it just seemed the cowboys outnumbered the cows!

Back in the day, there were hardly any fences or gates you had to worry about. The old cowboy had at times thought fences were more trouble than if they were not there. Fences made working cattle around the ranch much easier, but when trailing a herd down a dirt road, it was a lot more trouble than it was worth!

Trailing cattle in open country the old way was like moving water through the mountains, with a cow taking the easiest route, just like water. Now a cow needed to go places where it didn't want to go because of fences, and the cowboys had to trail them there.

Back in the day, there were also animals you had to worry about. That alone made cowboying interesting. There were wolves, coyotes, and grizzly bears, and you could do what was necessary to solve the problem without concern. Today you had to report the problem animal or take your chance with the authorities, which a lot of the natives did! The old cowboy always packed his Winchester for those occasions.

There was a time when a person could see elk or even a bear on the ranch. Now Walker had to be back at cow camp in order to see any of those animals. The old cowboy had to take the time to ride further back in the mountains to enjoy the old ways.

The new ways were of laws and saying the right thing at the right time—politics. That was what the old cowboy liked about the mountains and animals—no politics! There was harshness to the old way of life, that's for sure. But if you respected it, then you would get along just fine. The times were changing, and he wished that he could finish his life before they had completely gone away.

That respect was something the Kid had shown. Even though he seemed to be real green at ranching, he had not complained once of hard work or bad weather. Oh, he didn't like some of the things the natives ate, that's for sure!

The flatlander Kid hadn't even complained about where he lived. Walker had laughed to himself; the Kid had wanted to be by himself and moved in to that old part of the bunkhouse. Nobody had lived in that part of the bunkhouse for years, and for good cause. Hell, the gaps in the logs probably let the weather in his room when the wind blew in that direction! He had taken the time to clean it out and make himself a place to bunk. The Kid had shown some of the grit of the old ways, using what's there and somehow making it work for his purpose.

Now the old cowboy wanted to see if the flatlander could handle some of Old Mother Nature's bad weather trailing cows. The cattle drive was about halfway over, and the weather was going to change yet again. It had already rained, with the sun coming back out to dry things a little. You just could not predict what spring weather would do at this elevation in the mountains. A person could get everything and anything in the same day. You just had to wait, watching all that Old Mother Nature could throw at a cowboy trailing cows for the first time.

The Kid, riding Old Brown, had just dried out, and the rain looked like it was coming back. He thought he should try a piece of jerky and walk a while, stretch his legs before the rain decided to come back. He thought that Old Brown would probably like a break from carrying all the hotcakes anyway.

Soon after, the Kid saw some of the cows spilling through a hole in the barbed wire fence. Riding Old Brown in a lope, the Kid was smiling from ear to ear, slapping his rope on his chaps, with Walker on his way to lend a hand.

They both seemed to enjoy the break from the morning routine, working the pairs back through the fence. The two cowboys rode back to the drag, with the Kid still smiling from the little bit of excitement.

"Paul, that was fun!"

"Kid, that old pony had a lot of get up and go when I rode him."

"Old Brown was your horse?"

"Yes, after I had my stroke it was hard at first to do a lot of riding. I thought I would give the old war pony a break and finish working the stud here. Working with the stud gave me something I could do till things got better; he is as gentle a stud as there is. I really did not know what I was going to do with Old Brown. That old war pony needed a rider, and you two seem to get along fine."

"You should have seen him lope to get around the pairs. I just hung on."

The two cowboys walked their horses, working the drag, and then it started to snow. The snow was at the temperature of between rain and snow—wet. The wind was blowing into their faces, and that was trouble for the cowboys. The cows just wanted to stop and face the other away from the wind.

Walker left the drag, walking his horse till the Kid could no longer see him, about fifty feet. The Kid could hardly see the cows right in front of him. It was snowing and blowing so hard that the pairs were turning their backs to it, stopping in the road. No matter what the Kid did, the pairs wouldn't move. Heck, even Old Brown turned his back to the storm. The brim of the Kid's not-so-new cowboy hat had already started to fall from the weight of the snow.

Then it stopped snowing just as fast as it had started. The sun came out, with everything covered with an inch of brilliant white snow. The Kid shook the snow off his cowboy hat, smiling at what had just happened, and thought to himself, *These animals have been doing this all winter long.* The pairs seemed to know that the storm was over and it was time to get back to walking to summer pasture. No big deal. The Kid let Old Brown have his head. He wanted to see what the old pony wanted to do first.

The cows were starting to move again, with the herd getting to be stretched out quite a ways. The Kid had to work the drag hard, as the pairs sounded their dissatisfaction in catching up with the rest. Soon after, Walker and the rest of the cowboys at a distance came into view, with dogs trailing the horses. There were a few more of the smaller calves at the drag now, probably the last to calf.

Feeling the same tiredness, he decided to walk a little to stretch his legs, giving Old Brown time to rest. The sun was shining, and he thought it would help move the calves if he were to walk, getting down a little closer to his work. Then Old Brown and the Kid could work separately like Paul and his dogs, the Kid being the dog, of course.

The Kid hung the hackamore reins on the saddle, with Old Brown walking beside him on the road. The old cow pony was the best the Kid could have hoped for; he just followed along next to the Kid. While walking in mud and snow stretching his legs, the Kid slapped his rope on his chaps, speaking to the calves, "Hup, hup!" But they just were getting tired from all the walking and were bawling for their mommas. Even Old Brown thought he could nudge them gentle-like with his nose and maybe get them to go a little faster.

Wondering what Sam and Helper would do to get the little calves to go faster, the flatlander Kid let out his rope a little, flipping the end at the calves' legs. *POW*, the calf nailed it with a kick. Smiling, he could not believe the calf was that quick, and he tried it again; the calf kicked again, starting to move a little faster.

Then he stopped. He heard a sound, a unfamiliar noise for trailing cattle, he thought. As the old cowboy had taught him, he stood quietly and listened.

Eventually the animal, or in this case the cook, would make its presence known. Lunch. Smiling, he looked down the muddy road, finding a red station wagon making trenches in the road.

"Well, Kid, is trailing cattle what you thought it would be like?"

"June, I believe other than the bad luck with the weather, I am having a great old time!"

"Well then, get you something to eat and tell the others I'm here with the grub."

The Midwest flatlander Kid now looked like a traveling carpet bagger with all his clothes tied in and around the saddle of his horse. It was embarrassing for the old war pony. He had no idea how warm it had gotten to be, but he had long since taken off his slicker, tied in a tight yellow roll in the back of the saddle. His heavy coat was tied to the front of the saddle using the rope tie downs and breast rings, and his wet leather gloves were lying on seat of the saddle drying. Finally, his almost-new chaps were draped over the saddle, holding the gloves down.

The flatlander Kid cowboy was back at the drag, working with Old Brown. They had both so far been able to deal with all the different changes in the weather almost smiling. Walking in gumbo side by side, he was living the dream of almost being a real cowboy— well, not so much real.

The Kid had never kidded himself that doing what real cowboys did on a part-time basis necessarily meant that he was one. He just wanted to do as much as he could before going back to his old life and waking up from his dream. But for almost an entire day trailing cattle, living the dream had been a walk through the pages of a Louis L'Amour book, probably one of those Sacketts again.

The pairs were trailing down the road at a comfortable pace without too much trouble. Oh, there was always that one headbutter that wanted to somehow make it through the fence or even jump a cattle guard, making the Kid get back in the saddle.

Then, as if someone or something wanted to wake him from the dreamlike state of mind, there was another sound, like someone shooting a really big gun, *boom!* It was almost like his almost-dry clothes that were draped over or tied to the saddle were a sign for the weather to change yet one more time.

As the almost-real flatlander Kid cowboy looked to the sky for some natural sign that could have possibly made the noise or where the sound came from, drops of Mother Nature's spring rain hit him in the face. Oh not again! The Kid tried to measure the seriousness of just a couple drops, now maybe a few sprinkles. Then, as if Old Mother Nature had almost convinced him to relax, she let all the rain and lightning from her clouds above fall.

Similar to the heavy blowing snow earlier in the day, it was hard to see the cows from the downpour of rain. After putting his clothes back on the best way he could, the Kid decided to ride Old Brown, the real cow pony, the rest of the way to summer pasture.

Cow Camp

The old cowboy smiled with his heart of hearts, having a sense of relief that one more time he has proved to everyone and most of all to himself he can still do his job. Maybe there will be a day in the years to come that he won't be able to, but that day has yet to come.

After Walker had somewhat recovered from his stroke, the doctor said the life he so much loved was going to be something less. Maybe it was time to start taking life just a little bit easier. The doctor said probably that he could try to ride a horse that he could trust, maybe continue to ride Old Brown even. But the days of riding all the tough horses he was used to riding were over.

Let one of the younger cowboys ride them. Always there comes a point in a person's life when it is time to pass on his knowledge to others—maybe a kid.

The medical profession also said there would be no being alone for long periods of time. Make sure someone knows where you are at all times and what time that you are supposed to be home, so in the case you don't make it, someone will come looking for you. Walker had responded to the doc by saying, "Bullshit!" He wasn't going to act like some old person who needed to have someone change his diapers! There was a sorrel stud back at the ranch the cook had given him that needed to be topped off. So he was going to live the rest of his life like he always had, living today, 'cause there could be no guarantee of tomorrow.

After the old cowboy had spent enough time recuperating, he thought it was time to get back in the saddle. He used an old wooden box to step on, helping to get a little closer to the stirrup. As he stepped on the wooden box, making his way to the stirrup, the sorrel stud just stood patiently, waiting for the old cowboy to take all the time he needed. Always the sorrel stud stood still, seeming to help by leaning a little one way or another, helping the old cowboy get back where he belonged. Once in the saddle, the two were ready for a short walk around the main ranch.

After all the time recuperating, he was just now going to a place the medical profession said he would not be able to go by himself. It wasn't the first time Walker had proven that folks were wrong about him. Well, almost entirely in the wrong—after all the fuss, he did let himself have a little help with some of the chores at his cow camp, or is that entertainment, the Kid.

The two summer pastures, where the pairs would be grazing, were just a short riding distance from the old cowboy's cow camp. That's where the Kid would come in; the other pasture fence would need fixing like the lost the old Dodge pasture. Once the pairs had grazed the first pasture down, he needed some help to trail them to the other pasture. Walker now needed some help to do both, and his answer to all persons concerned about his health issues was the flatlander.

After the long trip, the old cowboy sat leaning back against his camp trailer in his favorite chair. Looking across the spring is the old cabin that is a museum of memories from all those years past. Someone had spent a lot of summers in that old cabin that now looked small and in tough shape.

The front of the cabin had a couple of license plates nailed on the logs that someone had found in the mountains over the years. There were horse shoes nailed to the logs to give the cabin that lived-in look. Also, there were a couple of steel traps that someone had used years ago. The traps just hung on the cabin, hoping that someone would use them after all these years.

Way back in the day, someone must have gotten bored and tried to get television reception at one time or another. The weather had taken care of that idea, or they simply found more interesting things to do. The antenna was still hanging in a bent mess of aluminum rods in case a person would like to try again for fun.

Smiling to himself, he tried to remember the last time he had taken a tour of the dusty bones from the past. There were two single bunks with a wood stove for heat and cooking. Pack rats had long since chewed up what had remained of the mattresses. They had built a few nests in the kitchen drawers and one big one in the flour bins. The cupboard doors just hung askew from their hinges, with the shelves having that old plastic stick tack paper lining them. There was still a almost-clean place for a wood stove that had been long since been taken away to the ranch and put in one of those places where all those things nobody knows what to do with go.

The old cowboy sat thinking the cabin was just another set of bones that shows the old pioneer days that he was sentimental about. It's a reminder to the old cowboy he used to be a part of the good old times, and that's nice. It had to be as sentimental to all the others that have used it over the years.

After all the time recuperating, the old cowboy was finally able to lean against the trailer in his favorite chair drinking coffee with his dogs by his side, looking to the ridges for some peace.

That night while lying in his bunk, the old cowboy was anxious for morning to come and to see what he could see. First he needed to check the cattle. Bulls were there now, and you never know what trouble those animals could cause. He wanted to ride the fence, making sure the Kid had it in good enough shape for the summer to hold all the cattle.

Once that was all done, he would just ride the ridges to let all the animals know he was back. He wanted to see if that young buck was still around. He wanted to play his game of keeping track of him. In a week or so, Walker wanted that buck for jerky.

The old cowboy liked to take the time to single out a particular animal, like the buck. He would find all the buck's favorite places and times when he would be somewhere—where the best grass is, where he likes to get water, where the mud holes are to roll in, getting away from the mosquitoes and flies.

There are all kinds of habits an animal has if you take the time to watch. And if you were good enough in the mountains, you could get to a good spot. Waiting for an animal to show up is the key to hunting. A person could get a close shot at a buck for jerky if he was to have the mind to take the time.

It was a great guessing game the old cowboy liked to play. Walker would stay still, seeing if the buck would notice him. If he was lucky, the buck would decide to lie down, maybe sleep for a while. That's when the old cowboy would take his shot, when the buck was asleep! He would get close enough to use his twenty-two rifle and pop the animal in the head. That left the meat clean of any shots, with the old cowboy in a good place to clean and gut the animal.

Walker had spent so much time riding horses in the area that he knew all the areas that the different animals would settle in. Some days he would ride for fifteen to twenty miles to see some of the old timers just to let them know that he knew they were still there, and let's play our game. It was comforting to Walker that he could still see what other people just talk about and that the animals seemed to give him the space to be there, almost like he was one of them, an animal in the mountains of Montana.

Maybe the Kid would be here long enough that he would show the flatlander how to hunt. He could learn to pack a horse and tie all the knots that would need to be used. The old cowboy thought the Kid would like to do that. Walker wanted him to know his way of hunting, old school!

The old cowboy was up and getting a little something to eat before the sun came up. The dogs were as anxious to get going as was their partner. He threw together some bacon and peanut butter to make himself a sandwich, one of his favorites. He tossed a piece of bacon to each dog, and out the trailer door they went!

The sun was starting to come up over the eastern ridges, taking a little chill off the morning. The early-morning glow gave enough light for him to tell the dogs to go get the horses, and he would have oats for the horses and a strip of bacon for each one when they came back.

The dogs ran off to find the horses, with Walker putting a couple of coffee cans of oats in each of the horses' feed tubs. He put on his chaps, spurs, and silk bandana while waiting for the horses to come in. As is the routine, the horses came in running after the dogs with tails extended from their hind quarters. The scene made the old cowboy smile broadly.

Walker saddled the stud. He wanted to be with the sorrel and his dogs on his first day back. The horse, for no older than he was, showed remarkable attachment to Walker. He acted like a horse that seemed to understand what was required of him because of the circumstances—patience.

Sam and Helper had been there for support, always finding some way to help see the brighter side of his troubles. The dogs would just do something as simple as grabbing at the bottoms of his chaps when he needed to feel a little love and attention. He just wanted to be with all of them when he looked for his old friend in the mountains.

Old Mother Nature seemed to be cooperating for his first day back riding to summer pasture. Her mosquitoes had yet to show their presence in abundant volume. That alone put a smile on his face.

After his morning of preparation, he started riding, checking for signs of what was around, as was his routine. Sam and Helper were ever-faithfully following, sniffing the air for any scent that might be there to investigate. Sam and Helper were the addition that Walker enjoyed. He was very adept at cutting and listening for sign. The dogs just had their noses going for them. They seemed always to know before Walker that there was something close by.

The four friends were methodically looking for signs and listening for sounds. If you're listening while keeping your pace slow with the intent on hearing sounds, it would surprise most people how much is there to hear. By doing that, it might keep you from running into a bear, or maybe something is stalking you at the same time. A person could never know in the mountains.

A bear, for instance, comes out of hibernation with an upset stomach. It has been hibernating for months, recycling its body fat and waste. That also translates into a coat that gives off a pretty bad odor that dogs can smell quite a ways away! The bear is also going to green grass to help settle its stomach, just like a dog. So a person could see a bear around green grass or check the breeze for its bad odor.

That right there is something else a person needs to keep track of all the time. The wind is always giving your position away, no matter how good a person is in the mountains. The animals are better at locating you, as it was intended by Old Mother Nature. They live in the mountains and have used what is available to them their entire lives. That is the game the old cowboy likes to play. He was betting from all the years he had been in these mountains that he was as good at locating them as they were locating him.

After awhile, he was riding the fence where the Kid lost the old Dodge, and the old cowboy started to laugh all over again. He was just thinking of that hotcake Kid all haired up, standing in the middle of the road with fence stretchers and pliers waiting to take the truck back. Walker thought to himself, *I would give the Kid his truck if I had it!*

Watching the pairs from atop a ridge, the old cowboy sat chewing tobacco, with his right leg bent around his saddle horn. The bulls were doing what bulls do: sleeping, pawing the ground to show how tough they are, and fighting. He thought it really did not give the best example of the male species; he smiled to himself at the thought.

As he was scanning the pairs for anything that might be out of sorts, he saw a calf that looked a little humped-up and stiff legged, pretty new compared to the older calves from February. He had better rope the little feller and give him some medicine.

As he got out his rope, uncoiling a loop, the stud horse was alert and ready to go. Walker could feel the muscles of the horse tense under him. He talked to him a little bit to get him to relax.

He walked the stud very slowly to face the calf, which was just looking all stiff legged and humped up from being sick. He had his loop resting on his shoulder ready to throw and the pigging rope in his mouth.

The calf was trying to figure out what to do, and Walker tossed his loop over the calf's head. The easy motion startled the calf a little bit, but the old cowboy walked his horse, just following the calf where it wanted to go till it stopped. After taking the slack out of the rope, he hard tied his rope to the saddle horn.

The old cowboy stepped down off the horse, following the rope to the calf. The little feller put up a little bit of a fight, but Walker was still able to grab him in his flank, laying him down on the ground gentle like. Then just like in all the rodeos, he took his pigging rope from his mouth, tying the calf's legs.

After giving the calf medicine, Walker waited till he saw the calf suck a little milk from its momma. Then he gave Sam and Helper some attention to say thanks for the help before stepping into the stirrups.

During the next few hours, Walker only found a few more to doctor, mostly the younger stuff. The calves had gone through a lot in the last few days—branding, the cattle drive, and bad weather. A few had scours, but all in all they had made the trip in fine shape.

The old cowboy was happy how the morning went. Now it was time to eat and watch a little, making sure the cows were the only thing in this part of the country. He took the time to review in his mind what sign they had come across on their way to the pairs.

At the beginning of the day, he followed the creek to a sandy bend with aspen trees. After a little ways, he found paw prints followed by a back and forth dragging impression print—a beaver.

As he continued to ride the creek, he came across tracks from a moose. After following all the signs, there off at a distance is a bull moose with his head submerged in the water, eating what he could find at the bottom.

Waiting, the old cowboy, with his dogs, watched as the bull moose finally lifted his head out of the water. Looking in all directions with water's green vegetation hanging off his rack, he smelled the intruders. Walker smiled, wondering whether at this distance the bull with his bad eyesight could tell if his old friend is back.

After they were done with eating, the old cowboy straightened the saddle on the stud and tightened the cinches. All was well with the pairs, and now he needed to go check out the next pasture the pairs would be moved to. This time he would take the higher route to the other pasture. The creek bottom had showed him a little bit of information. He would look in the trees and ridges for more.

The dogs paused, looked in the direction of some trees, and ran. The old cowboy knew what that was all about. Sam had never been able to not go after a porcupine, and he passed that habit on to his daughter! The two dogs treed the animal, receiving a few quills each for their efforts.

"OK, which one wants to be first? Sam, you're the troublemaker. Let's start with you."

Walker gently laid Sam down on his side, putting a knee softly on his neck from behind the dog's back, and the other leg was straddling the dog's chest. He gently lifted one of the Sam's lips where there were three quills starting to come through! Walker shook his head, telling Sam this was going to hurt a little, and pulled the quills out the rest of the way.

Walker had used a combination of iodine and bacon grease that he called purple medicine. It had not worked over the years as well on the dogs as it has on the horses, for obvious reasons—bacon grease. He spread a little on Sam's muzzle and let the dog up.

Walker repeated the procedure on Helper, with the daughter having a few more quills than her father. This seemed to be the case in other trouble as well. This was not what Walker had hoped for. After all the time spent in the mountains, he had just got a wakeup call.

Walker rode the stud to the other pasture a few miles, always looking for sign that his old friend was still around. The dogs were following close behind, feeling a little down in the mouth, to say the least. Walker rode the fence and found there was some to fix, enough for the Kid to come for a couple of days at least. He started to wonder how the Kid was doing. He could get into more trouble quicker than anybody, maybe except for the dogs! Maybe the dogs had rubbed off on the Kid. He smiled at the thought.

It was getting late. It had been a long first day back, and Walker decided to head on back to camp, settling in for the evening. There was an old companion that generally showed at meal times that wasn't there last night. His friend was just a little amusement to finish out his day that he looked forward to.

When approaching cow camp, he decided to see if he could sneak up on the mare and young gelding. The old cowboy's war party got upwind of the field, hiding in the timber's edge. The two unsuspecting horses were at the spring drinking water. They followed the tree line, getting as close using the trees as they could, sitting absolutely still, waiting for the right moment to reveal their position.

The mare and gelding were eating a little green grass at the spring's edge, and suddenly their heads popped up. The old cowboy with his war party came out of the gulch like a raiding party of wild Indians. The old cowboy was giving his war whoop, and the dogs were barking. The mare and young gelding started to run toward camp to safety.

The old cowboy, along with his dogs, was in the race to get to camp first, ahead of the mare and young gelding. All the horses were running with tails extended, with the dogs being left a little behind. The old cowboy lightly touched the ribs of the stud with his spurs. He hit another gear, scatting past the other two horses, yeehaw!

Walker waved his cowboy hat at the mare and gelding as he went by to his cow camp! They all arrived at a breakneck speed, making quick turns to keep from running into things, with the mare and young gelding crow hopping and bucking.

The old cowboy had to hang on to the stud like he was in a rodeo on a bucking bronco! The dogs came in, starting to heel what they could grab, and Walker called them all to settle down. The fun was over with, or was it just beginning?

He put the stud in the small corral, taking the bridle and saddle off, hanging them on the corral rails. After all the racing, he had to let everything cool down a little before he gave them their rolled oats. He turned the stud out, with all three horses running off, with the dogs running after them, leaving a big smile on his face.

The old cowboy thought he would eat outside and see if his old friend would visit. For supper, he thought cut-up potatoes fried in bacon grease sounded good with scrambled eggs mixed in. The cook had sent up a couple loaves of sourdough bread. He cut a couple of thick slices to go along with his meal to wipe the plate almost clean.

Outside, the dogs were back after a good day's work, patiently waiting by his chair. He set the plate full of food outside on his chair next to the trailer. He gave the dogs that, "Do not eat my food" look, and they, of course, turned their heads in disappointment.

The horses were watching him come in their direction and begun nickering their approval. He gave the horses their rolled oats and walked back to find his friend eating from his plate.

"I didn't think you would pass up fried potatoes and eggs. But you better take note that the dogs don't eat from my plate. Now let an old cowboy eat in peace!

"When Walker was done eating, he gave the rest to the dogs with a fork, letting the camp robber bird have the plate on the ground. He leaned back in his chair, waiting for the mountain sunset to unfold in all its colors, drinking his coffee. He heard coyotes barking to each other in the distance. Walker sat wondering about the cook and the Kid, smiling to himself. He would sleep well on this his first night back at his cow camp.

"Kid, you about done eating?"

"June, I have only just sat down!"

"Well, hurry if you want me to show you something about fishing."

"June, can't I eat first? What's the hurry all of a sudden?"

"Kid, I am in rush to get things all lined out to go fishing tomorrow with my mother, and you need to learn how to catch bullheads tonight before it gets too late to do it!"

Smiling, the Kid stuffed as much food into his mouth as he could while walking out the mudroom door. He was smiling because the fun-loving native (FLN) cook was about to teach him his first and probably most important lesson on fishing, the bait.

The FLN cook thought probably the most important lesson was to teach him how to catch her bait, bullheads. She thought it would be nice to get her fishing season started in the right direction. The FLN cook showed him what had become tradition among her family, how to use her very expensive, old, rusty, beat-up screen. It had most certainly become a treasured family antique handed down from her mother. It was just one of many of her prized possessions that helped her to get the most out of all the fishing days of summer.

The FLN cook was already halfway to the creek behind the horse barn on a mission. She was smiling from ear to ear.

Once the Kid had caught up to the FLN cook, she handed him her bullhead screen, telling him it was a valuable family antique, so be careful with it. Then she asked him a question, smiling that FLN cook smile that always meant trouble for him.

"Kid, you got your cowboy boots on?"

"Cookie, no way am I getting in the creek with my boots on. I'll just go barefooted."

"Trust the old cook, Kid!"

"Cookie, like that is ever going to happen anymore. I am still trying to get over all the graphic visualizations of Butkus' internal organs out of my mind."

After the sad attempt to get the Kid to go back in the creek wearing his almost-new worn-out boots from the first fun-loving old cowboy dunking, the lunatic for fishing FLN cook told the Midwest flatlander Kid all her detailed thoughts of how smart fish really are.

The FLN cook believed in her heart of hearts that fish are indeed smart. So if a Kid is to be serious about fishing, he needs to crawl on hands and knees, sneaking up to the creek, keeping low to the ground, no matter the obstacle, no matter the distance. In fact, fish can see a person, especially a really big hotcake-eating Midwest flatlander Kid. That most certainly is taking advantage of all the knowledge she was passing on to him. Respect is what the old cowboy had taught him.

Next the FLN cook believes in her heart of hearts that fish can hear everything a person says, especially a Midwest flatlander Kid who seems to be always talking to all the animals. In her mind, fish were a lot smarter than animals because they remember what is said, passing it on to the rest of their relatives, a fish network of sorts. So if you're saying anything important, like where you are going, the fish will always be gone when you show up there. Talking is really bad.

Last, never, never ever use your actual names, 'cause fish, especially the browns, remember who you are and will tell all their relatives. So when they see or hear a flatlander they can recognize, they go somewhere else, never coming back to this spot. There will be no more fish there.

"Oh you're a lunatic if you think fish can hear us! You know Paul told me you are just crazy about fishing."

"That old cowboy doesn't know anything about fishing. Now stop talking so loud, Flatlander, whisper!"

"Well, Cookie, I bet he doesn't think fish can hear, of all things."

"Flatlander, you are talking too loudly. You have to be quiet! I am telling you; the fish can remember faces and voices. Come on, Flatlander, work the screen like I taught you."

"Cookie, here's a question. We are catching bullheads for bait, a fish, to catch a trout, a fish, right? So, isn't that cannibalism, fish eating fish?"

Finally, she was pushed her to the limit. The FLN cook said, "Flatlander, do you ever shut up?"

"Cookie, I think I have stumbled on why all the natives around here are eating all the internal organs of the livestock. Everyone eats fish. You are what you eat, Cookie."

The Kid, with the FLN cook, worked hard at catching what they thought would be enough bullheads for the entire season. Of course, the exasperated FLN cook was on the creek bank shushing the flatlander, with the Kid, of course, making as much noise as he could, and asking the many technical questions that had been nagging at him. Cannibalism was just the first.

The FLN cook had finally had enough when the flatlander hotcake-eating Kid stuck his face into the creek, wanting to carry on a conversation with any fish that would listen.

"Cookie did you really think I would wear my boots in the creek?"

"I was hoping, Kid. Now show me how many you caught."

"Cookie, this should be a good start, don't you think?"

"Kid, that many should keep me and my mom fishing for a few weeks. There are always more bullheads a flatlander can catch. Here, give them to me so I can cut them up and put them in the freezer."

"Now what's my first lesson about fishing?"

"What do you mean, Flatlander? I just showed you how to catch your own bait."

"Oh, I get it, you just needed someone to catch you and your mother some bullheads."

"Well if you want, you can use a few of these when you go to see Paul at cow camp. I will even let you use my screen if you need to catch some more. But you have to be careful when using it. It's a part of my family's history. This screen has probably seen many good tourists like yourself catch bullheads for most of my relatives going back to the first homesteaders."

"Now you have and gone done it. Let's make our bet."

"Kid, didn't Paul tell you not to bet me? I have never been defeated."

"Yeah, he said something about that. I think it is time for someone to make you eat those words."

"OK, make it easy on yourself. Tell me your bet."

"Five bucks."

"You sure you can afford all much money?"

"Yeah, say what you like, Cookie, it's not about the amount of money. It's about the losing and handing over of the money, which just might kill you to know a Kid from the Midwest who has never lived here, a flatlander, can whoop another person, you, a FLN cook who has lived here all her life fishing. That would be quite a humbling life experience, wouldn't you think?"

"Kid, I think I would move out of the country and change my name to Flatlander. I am even going to give you a handicap. I will fish behind you, catching all the fish you don't. You can fish as long as you like, and I will be right behind you."

"Cookie, you're going to get whooped. Shall we say sometime midsummer then?"

"Why wait for defeat? Be a flatlander and take your medicine now."

"You would like that. I need to get started first perfecting my technique."

"You let me know the time and place. Hope your waiting won't make you chicken out. Now I have to start getting things ready to put in the station wagon for tomorrow. You can help if you want."

A couple hours before sunset, Walker rode his stud into camp looking to the old Dodge. He was glad to see the Kid had made his trip to camp without any trouble. The old cowboy looked forward to seeing the Kid. He had some catching up to do and some stories to tell.

While taking time to sit drinking this morning's warmed-up coffee with his old friend, the old cowboy smiled at the bird, putting a couple strands of his chewing tobacco in the coffee for more taste and just maybe to kill any worms he or the bird might have.

It wasn't too long after that when the Kid came running down the middle of the creek, acting like he was running away from something.

"What's the hurry about?"

"Paul, I wasn't going to stay long enough to find out. I was fishing and heard the willows start to break. I just got the heck out of there."

"Kid, I haven't seen anything around here that would be a problem. It's probably just that bull moose. The dogs will run him off. We can check for sign tomorrow.

After their days apart, the two friends were preparing food for their supper: venison and potatoes. Walker had the Kid start cutting some potatoes up while he went outside to get the fire started.

They sat around the campfire visiting about both of their weeks, and the talk turned to fishing while everything cooked.

"Go get your pole and I'll take a look at what you have."

The old cowboy helped the Kid tie leader on his line and show him how to tie a couple of knots that would probably not come out. He explained how to put the bullhead on and that he shouldn't wait to feel a big tug on his line. The fish nibble at the bait, so he shouldn't look at the line in the water to see if the fish are pushing the spinner around. He gave just a couple of tips to the Kid.

The camp robber came for a visit, landing on the ground in front of Walker while he sat listening. The Kid wasn't too interested until the bird jumped, landing on Walker's knee.

Smiling, the old cowboy picked out a couple strands of chewing tobacco from his pouch, dropping them in his coffee cup. The old cowboy winked at the Kid, saying, "It helps with worms to do it this way." The Kid looked at Walker with a big grin.

"That happens all the time, Kid, nothing to write home about."

"Paul, that bird just landed on your knee."

"The name of the curious bird is gray jay or camp robber bird. This one seems not to be afraid of people. This little fellow and I have been friends for a few years now. One day he just showed up. I let him eat off my plate and drink some of my coffee to help out with the worms. Better to be safe than sorry, I thought. Sounds like someone else I know."

"I promise not to eat off your plate. Plus, I have had enough chewing tobacco to last quite awhile. Hey, the dogs don't even bother the bird. Why is that?"

"I cannot answer that, except to say the bird doesn't eat that much, I would guess. Kid, the cook told me about you betting her."

"Yeah, after today I think I better get to practicing catching some fish."

"After we eat breakfast tomorrow, I show you some things. We can also check on what made all the noise."

"That would be great if you would. Otherwise I am going to get my butt kicked."

"Kid, that's going to happen either way. The cook is that good. I resorted to taking the dogs along, teasing her while she fished last weekend, just to give the fish a chance. She gets to catching so many I cannot eat them all. Over the years, I am surprised there any fish left in the creek."

"Then I am in big trouble. Paul, take a look at the damn bird. It's eating off my plate now. I have competition."

"Kid, the bird doesn't have a chance."

The two friends talked, ate their food, and cleaned up their dishes. One dog licked Walker's plate and the other licked the Kid's, all clean. They sat talking about their lives, telling funny stories of the years past.

"Since you are here with me, who is milking the old girl?"

"June went to do some fishing with her mom before the runoff gets too bad. The boss said he would be there to help out and for us to have a good time." "Really, the boss said that?"

"Yeah, what's the big deal?"

"Dear, sweet Buttercup doesn't get along with the boss. He is one of those types that are always in a hurry. You take that into account with you taking over the milking and the kittens, there could end up being casualties."

"The boss cannot be that bad at milking."

"Yep, he is!"

After all the good company, Old Mother Nature's daylight turned to night, with millions of her stars slowly coming to life surrounding a full moon. The old cowboy sat leaning back in his chair against the trailer, with Sam and Helper lying by his side. He had his coffee, and when that was gone, chewing tobacco would be his next choice.

The Kid sat cross-legged in his sleeping bag, eating jerky and drinking spring water. Off in the distance, there was an audience of coyotes barking to each other in excitement, waiting for the old cowboy to begin telling his stories of days gone past.

With an orchestra of soft sounds coming from the spring nearby, the stage was set for the Kid from the Midwest, a flatlander, to listen to stories told by a real cowboy around a campfire in the mountains of Montana.

Once the old cowboy had paused long enough, he told stories of trailing cows with the old man and his dogs. They would start the cattle drive at the ranch and trail the cows clear to the stockyards at Hamilton to sell them. There were not a lot fences to speak of, and a cowboy had to be schooled in the old ways to get there in one piece. They camped all the way under the stars, like tonight. The drive would take as long as it would take, depending on weather and any misfortunes that might happen on the way.

He told stories of driving freight wagons with mules, with the old timers using an air gun and jerk line to communicate to the lead mules. The old teamster would holler the mule's name, pop the gun, and give a tug on the line to get the mule to turn gee or haw. They hauled whatever someone wanted to freight, making a full load. But like the Kid, he had caught the tail end of freighting because trains and damn automobiles were taking over by then.

There were dangers you had to be able to handle. On the trail, an animal or individuals of less than having good manners could be just around the corner at any moment. Walker packed his Winchester for those occasions.

But the story he liked telling the most was about a wild horse the old cowboy had come across in his mountains. The stud horse had a coal black coat, long mane and tail, and white blaze on its face.

After trying over the years to get a close look, to tell the type of breed, at a distance Walker thought the wild horse was bigger than most riding stock and smaller than a work horse. He thought maybe it was a cross of a Morgan and something else.

The old cowboy would like to know where the stud came from. Where does he stay at different times of the year? How old he is? Are there more? Maybe the stud has a bunch of mares that he keeps. It would be a real shock if he had been there all this time and Walker had just found him.

That would be something to see in the mountains close to home—a herd of wild mustangs. Wouldn't it be great not to do anything but chase after them, feeling the excitement of riding a horse flat out running alongside of a bunch of wild mustangs?

The old cowboy talked of tracking the horse over the years. The horse was so smart at all the elements of living wild. The old cowboy had to use all of his abilities of tracking, keeping absolutely quiet, air movement, and scent, to get as close as he has so far to the horse.

He had thought about bringing a bunch of mares up and just turning them loose. The stud would surely want the mares for himself. Then he could just round up his mares with the wild stud and drive them all to a coral of some sort.

But then the game would be over, and what could anybody do with the stud? The stud represented how at one time he used to live—free. It was how, if he had his way, he would somehow get back to living. He was getting old and needed to feel free one last time before he was gone. The old cowboy hoped with all his heart he would get that last chance.

After all the time and effort of trying to catch the wild stud, the old cowboy decided finally that he should let the horse alone. The stud wouldn't make a cowboy a horse to ride. A cowboy wouldn't be able to break him or to work in a team of driving horses, so what was the point of catching him?

So he finally just had to settle for watching the wild stud free from all the domestic influences. The old cowboy thought the wild stud should stay in the mountains where he could stay wild, as Old Mother Nature had intended.

After the last of the wood had been put on the fire and the old cowboy had told his stories under moonlit skies, the Midwest flatlander Kid went to sleep all rolled up in his sleeping bag. He was thinking of cattle drives, driving horses, and most of all, running with wild mustangs on horseback.

Listening to the old cowboy tell his stories around his campfire on that first night was as fine an evening to this day as the Kid has ever spent.

Hairpin

Walker and the Kid had come a long way together. The flatlander Kid had only anticipated working for the summer, and then he thought he would go back to civilization, to his real life. Four years later, it had not worked out that way. The two friends were having so much fun, he had found it hard to leave the ranch way of life.

But one thing led to another, and all three friends had moved to a different ranch, the banker's ranch. The old cowboy had kept finding something the Kid wanted to try next, and the grays got him to make the move.

The Kid is still sentimental to this day about the old milk cow, Buttercup, the old brown horse, and the wild-ass cat, Ike, and all her kittens. They all had taught him so much. It was hard on the Kid to make the move from the place where it had all started.

Nevertheless, one of the hidden truths the Midwest flatlander had to learn from working on a ranch was that a hired man only had access to the animals as long as he stayed to do the work.

But all his fun at the time was generated from friendships that had developed from working around the native couple, so what else was he supposed to do but follow?

So after he had his own Dodge truck, with automatic transmission, loaded with his personal belongings, he started the process of building roots all over again.

The three friends had been working at the banker's ranch for a little over a year now. But as it has happened a few times before, another opportunity came his way to do something really special.

"Kid, this is what you always seemed headed for from the start. I'm happy for you."

"Paul, we have been around each other for what, about four years now?"

"Yes, I remember you were that big flatlander Kid who was only going to stay for the summer. You kept trying to kill yourself by playing with all the animals. I really find it amazing you are still all in one piece. Really, Kid, you have taken some big hits."

"But Paul, the time has really just flown by. It's still hard to believe I have been ranching for all this time."

"Kid you think your girl is still waiting?"

"Paul, I think that train has left the station, so probably not! Nan is still wondering what happened to me and even came out to the ranch with her sister, Marion. Both wanted to see what all the fuss was about.

"However, after all the fun I've been having with you and June, I really kidded myself that I would ever leave. Everyone thinks you and June have somehow persuaded me to stay with the ranch work, that someday I will come to my senses and get a real job. They cannot believe I am still working on ranches, and I cannot imagine going back."

"Yeah, you kind of lost track of that part of your life, but I think that's good, don't you?"

"Paul, that's what I am telling you. I have a dog just like Sam and Helper."

"Kid, to tell you the truth, that was the entirely June's idea to give you Dawg on your birthday. June and I talked about it just a little, you know to get you a pup for your birthday the first year. But at the time we did not know whether you were going to stay or go back to your old life. I told her that, and of course she had already had made up her mind on the subject.

"Thinking back on it now, I believe you two were able to grow up on a ranch together. Really neither one of you at the time knew what you were doing. June and I thought you might have liked some company figuring things out. You know, two heads are better than one. June and I will always call you the Kid with the Dawg."

"Paul, I have to admit Dawg is a lot of company. I've never seen an animal try some of the things he tries to get away with. You know he isn't much on cattle, but the darn Dawg did well at herding sheep. Dawg seemed to take to it."

"How did you like herding sheep?"

"I did not care for the sheep part. A band of almost five hundred is a lot to handle for someone who was just starting out. The old Pueblo Indian, Billy Chawewe, I worked with knew what he was doing but could not speak a word of English, making it hard for me to catch on to things.

"What I really enjoyed was herding the sheep up through the Centennial Valley past Lima Dam. That is probably the most beautiful place on earth for me to have been working. We both had our individual sheep wagons to cook, eat, and sleep in. Paul, I just worked on the horses, fished, took baths in the creek, and had this little wood cook stove in the sheep wagon for cooking."

"As big as you are, how did you fit in the sheep wagon?"

"Paul, it was pretty crowded. The bunk was a narrow six feet long, and the ceiling was about six feet at the crown of the canvas. So I just camped outside when the weather was good using your canvas and used the sheep wagon for really bad weather."

"How did you like the goats?"

"Paul, the goats were hard to catch, the milk smelled and was awful to the taste, so you can have the goats."

"But the three horses I worked with were fun. I would ride one in the morning and change to another horse in the afternoon, with a horse having a full day off to recover from the previous day's work.

"There was a raw-boned roman-nosed gray gelding that I had to ride. Paul, that horse would buck for what seemed to be the longest periods of time without a break. Sometimes I would try to put him in water or a bog just to make it harder for him to buck. Finally I just accepted his bad disposition, trying to stay in the saddle. But once he knew you were there to stay in the saddle, he was fine. I never understood why he was the way he was. It would have been good to have you take a look at the gray to see what you thought. Maybe I was doing something to set him off.

"Now, Paul, the second horse, a sorrel mare, you couldn't catch. When she knew you were afoot, there was no way you could catch her. She was kind of spoiled that way. I eventually had to saddle one of the other horses to catch her. Then once she saw you coming on the other horse, she would come in. She knew you had her then.

"But Paul, my favorite horse of the three was the bay gelding from the flats back east. This horse had never been out of a barnyard, never seen a mountain or even drank out of a creek. I think that darn horse was so happy just to be doing something; he followed me everywhere, like a puppy dog. He spooked and tripped over everything, it didn't matter what. If the bay saw a gopher, I'd give him his head, letting him get as close as he could before the gopher went down its hole. Paul, that darn horse wanted to check out the hole the gopher went down. That horse was a riot.

"Now Paul, when I first tried throwing a loop from the bay, he was fine till he saw the rope come into view. My God that horse side stepped so fast. He almost left me in the air standing!

"So come evening, I would tie his halter rope to a post in a fence line. Then on foot, I got about ten posts away and started throwing some loops on the posts. The bay would watch with his ears twitching back and forth, listening to all that was going on. When he was comfortable, I would move a post closer. That went on for about a week. Then the day when it was his turn in the rotation to work, I would throw some loops from the saddle. It didn't take long after that for the bay to get over the rope.

"Paul, as you know, I had only ridden a few horses up to that point, and then only with you close by if I had problems. These three horses were the first I had the chance to work by myself. Paul, it was a lot of fun to practice what you have showed me over the time we have spent together. I can really see how a person can get caught up in working with horses for a living."

"Kid, the individual that hired you to herd the sheep owned those horses. He could always ride a pretty tough horse. But look at what you got to do, herd a band of sheep up the Centennial Valley for what, about seven weeks. You had a sheep wagon to sleep in and three of the best horses to ride after you worked out your problems with them.

"Kid, after we left the old man's ranch, you had the spare time before you made the move to the banker's ranch. I thought it might be something for you to try. It sounds like you had a good time, and you have another line for your resume."

"Paul, after all the time that has passed, would you tell me something? How did I end up with riding a horse that used to be bucking stock from a rodeo? And by the way, that horse is the ugliest animal I have ever seen, and I named him accordingly too, Ugly. I have yet to see anything that matches his disposition, tough."

"You two are made for each other, and look how much you have learned from the old war pony. Since the first day we met, you could always seem to get along with the best of the worst animals. Remember your dear, sweet Buttercup?"

"Paul, Buttercup was all right. You taught me I had to respect the animal. Paul, I know I'm not the sharpest knife in the drawer, but I am sharp enough to know that old cow could have kicked my butt anytime if she would have wanted to.

"You told me once that if an animal is tough to get along with, then chances are it is because of the person, not the animal. All I had to do is find a way to make friends and build trust with the old milk cow. I will take as many of those animals as I can find. I think that is what you did with me, give me a place to hang out not having to look over my shoulder all the time."

"Kid, I just know from growing up on the reservation that people can be pretty damn awful. Now, you still need to tell me how you worked your flatlander magic on old Ugly."

"First you need to tell me how I ended up with that ugly white horse."
"You wanted him and the banker finally gave him to you is all."

"Nah, Paul, there is more to it than that. It just seems that after all this time that has passed, there have been people helping me get where I am today."

"Kid, I won't confess to anything that the cook has done or is still doing. Now your ugly horse's real name is Santos. The banker got him from a friend at the rodeo, just maybe to have a little fun with the cowboys at the ranch. Some of the cowboys started getting banged up, and really no one wanted to ride the old white war pony. You saved the horse from getting canned."

"Paul, I just thought it was a shame to can the horse and make a couple of bucks on the deal. The banker has plenty of money, and I wanted to try to ride the old war pony. After working with the three horses herding sheep, I wanted to see if I could finally use what I learned from you, thinking old Ugly would be a good test. Do you remember when I walked him to the house to show him to you?"

"Yes I do, I asked you what in the heck you doing with that ugly horse."

"You gave us our name of Double Ugly."

"Kid, I was only kidding about the name. It's just that June has always liked giving you heck about your hair. Since you have been ranching, how often do you shave and get a haircut?"

"Paul, it's not like I go to town a lot. And I'll be damned if I will let the cook get close to me with a pair of scissors."

"Yeah, that might be a bad thing to do. Can't blame you there. But let's get back to the horse. How did you win the old war pony over?"

"Do you remember the first day I tried to ride the old bucker?"

"Yeah, that gag bit should have never been put in the horse's mouth. That cowboy was having some fun with a flatlander. You were lucky not to get hurt."

"However, after I took the gag bit out of his mouth and used a hackamore, Ugly was fine. I had a little trouble catching him at first and finally had to put him in a small field by himself, away from everything else—no horses and absolutely no people. I would come to visit every morning before breakfast with a horse brush and a coffee can of rolled oats, with him always walking to the farthest point away from me in the field.

"When he would stop and look in my direction, I poured the oats in his feed bucket. Each day, he got a little more lonesome for company and a little closer to me.

"Dawg really helped to get Ugly to come the last few steps. When Ugly was that distance where a person just wants to try to grab his mane or even throw a loop to catch him, Dawg went up to him as if to say, 'The Kid is all right, come few more steps and get your brushing.'

"Paul, that is as hard a thing as I have done, waiting like you taught me to do. Never approach any animal first, always let them come to you first, no matter how long it takes. But you're right, once old Ugly came to me the first time, I never had a problem catching him after that.

"Paul, you want to know what I did to be able to ride that old bucker? Anything that reminded him of the rodeo, I stayed away from. I quit wearing spurs, never used my boot heels on his shoulders or his flank—all that stuff just reminded him of the rodeo."

"So now, Kid, you have anything but a cow dog, Dawg, Ugly the rodeo horse, and your draft horses Lucky and Rocky. They all seem destined to be somehow together trying to get your work done. I believe the bunch of you are just in it for the fun of being together to make things happen."

"I probably have to agree with you there. We all have a lot of fun being together. But Paul, I ended up with the best two draft horses anybody could hope for in Rocky and Lucky."

"Yes, I remember taking you to see them the first time. I believe things were at that time going downhill for all of us at the old man's ranch. I thought it might be the time to make a change and work somewhere else."

"Paul, you had been there over forty years. It is none of my business of the details of your disagreement with the boss. That's just a long time to work somewhere is all."

"Well, Kid, you're right about that. I was just thinking it would be something fun to do. The banker took the time to tell me he wanted to get back to as many of the old ways as possible. I thought to myself, 'How many more chances am I going to get to do that before I die?'"

"I still remember when you took me to see the grays. Dawg and I got out of your truck, walking to the fence, wondering what you wanted to show me. When I looked out in the field, there they stood side by side, looking at me. Do you remember what you said?"

"Yes, I said there is something more your size. See if you want to butt heads with those big guys."

"To this day, I am never going to believe I could be paired up with any animals that are a match for me like those two. I walked up to them thinking how a horse could be so big. Heck, their feet are huge. Paul, I stand six feet six, and their heads are over mine quite a bit.

"Paul, their personalities are so different. Lucky is all about work, and Rocky is all about playing. They are almost a matched set of horses as far as looks. Rocky has a more pronounced Roman nose than Lucky and is a little narrower at the shoulders. Other than that, they are the same.

"You showed me how to harness them and all the terms that a person uses, like gee and haw. When I hitched them up for the first time and saw how much power they have pulling a load, wow!

"If a person takes the time to line the horses out first, getting them both to lean into the harness, taking their first step in unison, it is almost as fine a thing as I have ever seen. Sometimes when I have loaded the hay wagon a little heavy, they have to get down low and scratch to get the load started. That's when you see the strength of the grays in pulling a load."

"I can still see you are excited about the grays. Did anybody tell you where they are from?"

"Paul, no, nobody has. I really had not thought about it till now."

"The grays are from a Canadian commercial hitch from one of the provinces. The banker said they were run in an eight-up hitch. You have been driving the grays in two and four abreast hitch."

"Yes, eight-up are like the horses pulling a stage coach but more."

"That's right. The banker thought since the grays are twelve to thirteen years of age, they would be good horses to teach someone like yourself to drive a hitch. One way or another, he needed to teach individuals like you to drive or find teamsters who already had the knowledge. I also believe the banker thought a person could salt and pepper them with young horses and it would help teach the young horses their job. Besides, I do not think there is a way to get the grays too excited about anything. They're pretty safe."

"You two still talking about horses? I thought it would be fun to eat at home and reminisce. But it looks like you two have already started telling stories without me," June said.

"June, we were wondering when you were going to show up with the grub."

"Kid, I haven't starved you yet, have I?"

"No, but over the years I have eaten some pretty strange stuff."

"Yeah, yeah, Flatlander! You two get washed up and come get some food."

The cook liked her job at the banker's ranch. She was making more money and had a remodeled cookhouse. The banker had even asked her to help in the new design. There were all-new appliances, a commercial gas stove, a walk-in cooler, and an island with a cutting board for a top. Above the island, all her pots and pans hung at a height she could reach easily. The place was pretty uptown, to say the least.

When they left the old man's ranch to work for the banker, they were all excited about the move. The banker had bought the main ranch and the Hairpin to make it as much the Old West as possible. The buildings were mostly restored, including the bunkhouse and horse barn, to look like the Old West. The ranch was going to have a few thousand head of cattle, so there was going to be a big crew to cook for and a lot of stock animals to take care of, including riding and draft horses. They were all excited to be a part of the process. The move had been a good fit for all three.

The three friends sat at the table eating the food the cook prepared especially for the Kid. It was the middle of January, and the Kid was going to be gone for the rest of the winter.

The banker was in the process of remodeling some of the old buildings at the Hairpin. The cookhouse so far was the only one his crew had the chance to finish because of the harsh winters there.

The couple he hired to take care of the bulls for the winter had not worked out, so the banker asked June if she thought the Kid would be able to do the job. The cook told the banker she thought the Kid was crazy enough that he would probably like living in Big Hole Valley in the middle of winter. She thought if it would be all right, that she and Paul would talk it over first with the Kid. They wanted to let him know what he was getting himself into. The banker said fine, but if he was going to do it, he had to commit to the rest of the winter, probably through the end of May.

The cook had gone home to visit with Walker about the Kid spending the rest of the winter at the Hairpin. The old cowboy thought it was just the right place for the Kid. He had never minded any part of the cold weather. It seemed to be just the opposite, in fact. The worse the weather, the more he seemed to have fun. He would be by himself and would probably take all his animals with him. The work would be hard feeding 250 bulls, but the Kid had taken to the hard work at the ranch just fine.

That evening after supper, they all sat at the table to discuss the move. This was the first time in all the lines on the Kid's resume that they really had a genuine concern about his safety. The Kid had shown a lot of enthusiasm with all the different areas of ranch work. Just since he had been at the banker's ranch, the Kid had developed into a pretty good teamster and could ride Ugly without too much difficulty. He also could drive draft horses in two up, four abreast, and was one of the cowboys who trailed a thousand head of cows from the main ranch to the Hairpin riding old Ugly. Those were all good signs the Kid had come a long way.

It hadn't meant too much at the time to the Kid, but he now could run just about any piece of ranch equipment on the place, from four-by-four tractors and buck rakes to balers. He had come a long way from his first days when he hadn't driven a vehicle with a clutch.

The old cowboy and the cook wanted to make sure he had all the facts about what he was getting into at the Hairpin.

"June, I cannot remember when there has been a time that you two were concerned about my health."

"Kid, the Hairpin, even though it is only just over the mountains in another valley, is a lot different from here. You are going to move there in the middle of winter and need to be aware of what the winter can be like."

"June, it cannot be that much colder than here."

"Kid, the temperatures can get well below zero. Then you have the wind chill on top of that."

"Paul, I have been fine here at temperatures at fifteen to twenty-five below zero. How much colder can it get in the Big Hole?"

"Kid, I have seen it get fifty to sixty below without the wind chill, staying there for days, even weeks at a time. Here we get cold for a few days and the temperature goes back up a few degrees. I would have to admit either place can get really cold. It's just the Big Hole Valley does it more as a rule than the exception."

"Paul, then how do the animals deal with the cold? They're out in it all the time."

"You can say what you like about a cow or a bull, the animals are probably one of the toughest animals around. Cows get pretty savvy to how to stay warm. They go to willows for cover from the wind and huddle up together as a group to keep warm. But you have to keep them fed. When it is that cold, their bodies burn a lot of calories to stay warm. They should have access to as much hay as they can eat in a day."

"Paul, then I must be feeding with horses. I cannot imagine any piece of equipment running in those temperatures."

"Kid, we will see when you get there. I would imagine you will take your grays and Ugly."

"Paul, I not going anywhere without them. Are there any horses there already?"

"Kid, the banker said there is a set of roan draft horses named Sunny and Red and a little bay horse for riding. Are you getting enough to eat, Kid?"

"Yeah, thanks, June, but you two make this sound like my last meal."

"We are not trying to talk you out of anything. It is just the Big Hole Valley is a different kind of place is all. You will be by yourself in one of the toughest places I have ever been in the winter."

"June, how will I get food?"

"The banker has remodeled the cookhouse, and I have already filled the walk-in cooler with meat and frozen food and the pantry with dry goods. That should hold you over for a while. There is a two-way radio to check in with, so you have to call us here at the cookhouse every night when you are done with your day feeding. That is something you have to do. If you do not make the call, we will know that something is wrong. Then we will send somebody else to finish feeding and find you when the snow clears in the spring."

"Yeah, thanks a lot there, Cookie. Now that you bring up snow, how much is there in the Big Hole Valley?"

"Kid I have been there when you couldn't see any of the fence posts on the level. You are going to a place that if you like the white stuff, it is paradise."

"Paul, I do like the white stuff. But if there is that much snow, how will I get in to the ranch?"

"Kid, the banker had one of the hired men open the road in with the D-6 cat, allowing me to take the groceries to the cookhouse. He had the operator leave it at the front gate in case it snowed any after he had plowed. If you decide to go, we have to call him to check on the road."

"Cookie, what do you mean if I decide to go? I am there already. Let's leave tomorrow morning."

"Seems like you have already decided."

"Paul, I talked it over with Dawg, and we decided it would be great to be with Rocky, Lucky, and old Ugly away from all the people at the ranch. I like it at the banker's ranch well enough. But since the three of us haven't spent that much time together, I would rather be by myself at the Hairpin, away from all the business at the main ranch."

"Yeah, I hear what you're saying, Kid. I am cooking for about ten hired men. That in itself doesn't lend much time for catching up with folks. Besides, when we were at the old place, you always were out and about by yourself, stirring up what trouble you could get yourself into. I think the Hairpin could be the place you could call heaven if you want to continue to get into trouble."

"I sure hope so, June. I have only been to the Hairpin once, driving cattle to summer pasture from the main ranch. Once we trailed the cows through the front gates, we loaded the horses in the trailers and drove home. Hey, there's something I did not know. There is a ghost town close to where we trailed the cattle."

"Kid that ghost town is the first state capital of Montana, Bannack. State or federal agencies maintain it for tourists. There used to be a hanging tree that the law used to hang flatlanders who were having too much fun."

"Yeah, yeah, Cookie. You know I am going to have to set a little time aside to check that place out. It would show how a town actually looked like in the old days. But let's get back to the Hairpin. What's its history?"

"I think the first thing that should be said is this: not a lot of people have been on the place for a long time. The old native that the banker bought the ranch from was to say the least an absent owner. He had a couple of hired hands who tried to make sure the perimeter fence was able to hold the cattle on the property. That made it possible to let the cows roam between the main ranch and the Hairpin, using the leased forest service land.

"The Hairpin for the most part has been cut off from people for a lot of years. It has to have animals aplenty. As you get the chance to go farther back in the ranch, there is a old cow cabin and three old homestead buildings that still are somewhat standing erect. Take into account all those facts with the place surrounded by the mountains covered deep with the white stuff you like so much and it has to be as close to living by yourself as you can get—paradise even."

"Well, Paul, I think that sounds like a good place for me and my animals."

"One more thing you're going to need something for protection. I want you to take my Winchester and a box of shells, just in case you have to shoot a coyote or two. Like I said, the place should be full of animals that may think nothing of trying to eat your Dawg."

"Paul, thanks. I really don't know what to say."

The next morning, excited to be on another adventure, the trip to the Hairpin was giving the Kid time to reflect on a lot of things. The thought of Walker letting him use his old Winchester was making the Kid proud of their friendship. He thought since the first day the old cowboy had taken him under his wing, watching over him. Now the old cowboy's Winchester was leaning on his seat as he drove in his old Dodge pickup with its automatic transmission.

The road to the Hairpin goes by the old ghost town Bannack, Montana's first state capital. When winter was over, he would have to check for the tree that the law used to hang flatlanders. He smiled thinking about the cook kidding him about that.

There was a reason not to go: the cook's food. He had just realized it was going to be a long time before he got to eat anybody else's cooking except his own. June had even given him one of her old cookbooks to use, marking some good recipes for him to try. Once the store-bought bread had been eaten from all the peanut butter and jelly sandwiches, he would have to bake some of his own bread. She had marked a page in the cookbook for that purpose. Then she had kidded him about doing his own cooking and had loaded up on peanut butter and jelly in the pantry, just in case things got a little out of control.

As he drove his Dodge past the old state capital a few miles, he noticed a real old cemetery to his right. It would be another thing to put on his list of things to check out when he had the time.

He started thinking of all the historic landmarks that Paul had talked to him about. He had just driven past Bannack, the first state capital that he had trailed cattle by, and Lewis and Clark's trail up at the lost old Dodge summer pasture at Lemhi Pass. But somewhere on the other side of the Big Hole Valley, going through the little towns of Jackson and Wisdom, is the Big Hole Battleground where army soldiers and Indians fought it out. Cool!

He drove through the Grasshopper Valley and over Carol Hill. Then, after a few more miles, he found the turnoff to the Hairpin using the parked D-6 cat as a marker. As the old Dodge's tires squeaked on the snow-packed road, the Kid felt a sense of adventure tugging on his mind. What a moment in the Kid's life! The plowed snow was as high as his pickup, so there was no turning back now. He smiled at his Dawg.

He noticed as he drove through the main gate that there were two roan draft horses watching his arrival. "Well Dawg, this is going to be our home for the rest of the winter. Let's check the place out."

As he stepped out of his old Dodge pickup, he realized the temperature was below zero. His nose hairs were freezing, always the first sign. He quickly puts on his stocking cap, winter coat, and choppers or mittens.

Dawg was fine, all haired up with his winter coat and red bandana tied around his neck. Walker thought since Dawg looked so much like a coyote, he should tie something colorful around his neck and maybe keep him from being shot by natives if he were to run across any.

First they walked directly to the corral off the barn, wanting to check out the roan horses. The horses looked to be bigger than the grays and not as friendly, although the horses were still very curious, sniffing the air with ears twitching. They kept their distance, watching every move the Kid and his Dawg made. Smiling, the Kid kept on walking, leaving them alone to compare their notes on the strangers.

As he opened the sliding barn doors, he turned on the lights to find the place a mess. From the first day of ranching, he had liked a clean barn and would have a fine time cleaning this one.

As he walked through the dim-lighted barn, he saw harness with horse collars hanging off pegs in front of individual stalls. The tack room was mostly empty except for a barrel full of oats and a few odds and ends. He would have a place to put all his tack that he had acquired up to now: saddle, bridles, horse blankets, curry combs, shoeing supplies, and tools.

While standing, he saw there were only six stalls with feed bunks, a few stalls short from the main ranch's barn. It was more like the old barn where he milked old Buttercup. Nonetheless, he had plenty of room for what he needed to do. He noticed off the tack room was a flight of stairs that led to the loft, where hopefully there was enough hay and straw stored for the rest of the winter.

After checking the barn, he found a 2440 John Deere tractor in a garage of some sort with the block heater plugged in. That made the Kid feel a sense of relief. He had started with the model bigger, 2510, on his first day of ranching with Walker. It had the same type of loader, with bucket and hooks that let a person grab a bunch of hay.

As he walked around the garage, he saw it was just big enough for the tractor to be backed in and close its doors. The Kid felt fortunate to have the garage. It would help keep the tractor out of the weather on those really cold temperatures. In the garage, there was a mixture of miscellaneous tools hanging on the wall over a narrow bench. On the wall opposite the tools was a wall having those little square wooden box openings full of all different types of nuts, washers, and bolts.

Upon entering the cookhouse, he found the place looked in order. He thought, *This is strange after all the mess at the barn. It's a good surprise.* Then he saw half a dozen jars of peanut butter and jelly with a note from the cook sitting on the table.

"Kid I tried to clean it the best I could with what time I had available. It was a shame to see a newly remodeled cookhouse in such bad shape. I know from being around you how you like a clean barn. You will probably keep this place a whole lot cleaner than the others folks did, June.

"Postscript: check out all the lunatic food Paul and I thought you might miss. On some of the jars we even put dates as best we could remember. Enjoy."

The Kid grinned, wondering what that was all about. A person could never know when the cook would try to have a little fun at his expense.

"Second postscript: here also is enough peanut butter and jelly for all those times you think you need to eat a flatlander sandwich."

The cookhouse was the best digs the Kid had on any ranch up to this point. It had a full kitchen with a big refrigerator-freezer filled with everything imaginable, a big gas cook stove, dual sinks with hot and cold running water, and a dishwasher.

The Kid had never used a dishwasher before. But from all the folks he knew who had one, they seemed to think that if you didn't load them right, bad things could happen. He would have to think about using it. It looked a little difficult anyway with all the buttons and lights. There were also plenty of pots, pans, and all the eating cutlery he could have imagined using. Maybe he would use the dishwasher after all.

On his way to the pantry, he found what had to be the best surprise yet. Besides the kitchen, the cookhouse had indoor plumbing, meaning an indoor bathroom. Yeah! He flushed the toilet and ran a little water in the sink just to make sure they both worked. He looked at himself in the medicine cabinet mirror, saying loudly, "Yes I have a bathroom!" Dawg lapped a little water from his newfound water bowl.

The Kid looked around, finding the pantry and walk-in cooler. "My God, June has lost her mind. The pantry has to be loaded with a grocery store full of dry goods. Everything imaginable is here!" On one side of the pantry she had stocked canned goods on shelves— corn, broccoli, asparagus, green beans, and rollers, better known to the Kid's world as peas, and cauliflower. He hates cauliflower.

Then, of course, he found cans of fruit—pears, ooh, cling peaches, those are so good on French vanilla ice cream, and a few small bags of red delicious apples. Cookie (FLN) had even faced the cans labels out so that the Kid could see what was what and had left a note on the canned vegetables. "Kid, I am going to try to stop smoking this winter, so you need to eat your fruits and veggies." There was a little smiley face written as her signature. "Postscript: keep that damn Dawg out of the pantry and walk-in cooler." Smiling at his Dawg, the Kid said, "How did she know you were in here?"

Now this is when things started to get really funny. As the Kid turned to see what was on the shelves opposite of all his fruits and veggies, he saw random sizes of jars of his favorite delicacies. To the flatlander Kid's horror, there were pickled pig's feet, cow eyes, which were new, a cow's heart, a cow's tongue that looked real, or at least in its natural state floating in whatever she used to pickle them, and of course last in the pantry of horrors were the ever present calf balls.

The jars were all lined up with labels of identification in combination with the name of his favorite linebacker where applicable. Picking up one jar that had just two calf balls, he started reading the label: calf balls, Kid's first branding and the date. This is when the Kid just lost it, thinking, *No way, Cookie, that's been four years ago.*

Laughing, the flatlander bent down to show his Dawg. "Look what I can do." He was thinking, *Those are about the best two friends, always making sure I have internal organs and my first castrated calf balls, almost like trophies of some kind.*

The Midwest flatlander Kid also smiled to himself, thinking he no longer needed to cowboy up to eat those delicacies. Dawg would get all that cuisine now. That was going to be one of the wonderful benefits of having a lunatic Dawg. He could have all the lunatic food now that they were alone.

Opening the freezer door, he found not just more but a lot more frozen food—hamburger, steaks of all sorts, hams, and his favorite frozen breaded shrimp. Between it and the pantry, the Kid surely wasn't going to starve to death. But there was something missing, and it nagged at him as to what.

Following his would-be cannibal Dawg, he walked the distance beside the long kitchen table to the bedroom. He almost got choked up seeing all the furniture. The room was almost self-contained, with a full-size double bed a with dresser, couch, and reclining chair next to a table, with an old radio sitting on top, just like an apartment.

Then if that wasn't enough, there was a full-size bathroom with a shower, with Dawg already taking another water sample from his second water bowl. The Kid thought he was surely in paradise now. He would have two bathrooms to use, one for him and one for Dawg if he had a mind to. He smiled at the thought.

It didn't take long till the Kid was done moving in and ready for something eat. Anxious to get outside to see what the rest of the place looked like, he decided on a peanut butter and jelly sandwich.

Then he remembered what food was missing, a staple in his diet of necessities. Where in tarnation was the jerky? He looked at his cannibal, bathroom bowl–drinking Dawg in desperation for help in locating the health food. "Use your nose."

Then he remembered in the huge refrigerator there was a big package wrapped in freezer paper. After opening the package, he found a note. "Kid I had nothing to do with all the shenanigans in the pantry. Enjoy the jerky from another buck we hunted together, Paul."

The two friends walked out of their new home, each eating a piece of jerky with their PB & J sandwiches, wondering what to do first and where to start.

He pulled the tractor out of its garage, finding a plowed road out of the back of the ranch buildings toward the mountains. The tractor went across a small bridge and then a short distance through a single jack-leg gate, and he quickly found the bulls.

There were three different types of bulls: black angus, Hereford, and one he had not planned on being there, a Texas longhorn.

The Kid shook his head at the sight of all the panels lying broken on the ground. It was a mess from as many of the 250 bulls that could squeeze into the stack getting something to eat.

Dawg was about three years old now and had been building a pretty good reputation as being a tough dog, but at this time, it should be said he was not a tough cow dog. Being a shepherd/husky cross, he didn't have a lick of cow sense. After three years, Dawg still went for the head and not the cows' heels.

After all the grief that the bona-fide cow dogs, Sam and Helper, gave Dawg about being the new kid on the block, Dawg had a little bit of a bad attitude. In fact, the only things Dawg didn't show his disdain for were his Kid and his horses, especially his horse, Ugly. The Kid had never seen a dog and a horse get along so well together and had thought more than a few times that it was Dawg who convinced the old Ugly not to buck him off.

Having worked with all the bad actors made the Kid wonder if maybe he had been given the life quest to somehow keep them from being shot or canned, which the case of old Ugly surely would be if the Kid had not stepped in. It did make for a lot of excitement that the Kid always enjoyed. It was almost like they were his own adopted family of anger-management misfits.

He fed the bulls enough to get them through till the next morning. The longhorns were still in the stack yard. There were too many for Dawg to move by himself, so the Kid lowered the bucket of the tractor, going bucket to head with the Longhorns. Dawg decided to help out by staying under the bucket, grabbing as many noses as he could. The combination had the Longhorns at a disadvantage, and the bulls decided to start leaving the stack yard one bull at a time. There, of course, is always one that has to try to make things difficult, and this was no different from any other situation.

The longhorn bull was by himself in the stack yard, really ignoring all the efforts to get him out. The Kid revved up the tractor, with Dawg under the bucket hitting the bull from behind. The bull turned to meet his attacker face to bucket, with the Kid smiling at the situation.

The Kid and his Dawg were amazed at how much longer the bull's horns were compared to the bucket. They faced off at each other, horns to bucket, and the Kid was grinning. He, of course, found the bull could use his horns as a weapon against the bucket. Now laughing at the situation, he used the loader as if they were his horns in battle, with Dawg grabbing at the longhorn's nose.

The next thing the Kid saw was his ever-faithful Dawg flying out the stack yard. A little big-eyed and laughing, he waited for Dawg's reaction. Dawg hit the ground in a heap, and as quickly as he left, he came back like a crazed animal looking to take revenge. The Kid felt proud of his Dawg. The little shit always seemed to find a way to come back to an altogether higher level of tough.

Between the renewed commitment of both the Kid and his Dawg, the longhorn bull ran out of the stack yard kicking, with Dawg and the tractor close behind. The Kid gave his Dawg a quick going over, just to make sure he was all in one piece, scratching his ears and rubbing his belly and that spot Dawg likes best, the top of his back close to his tail.

The Kid had a good afternoon, and it was time to get back. The sun was starting to go down, with the temperature dropping quickly. He would somehow have to find a way to open the next stack yard. Feeding this many bulls was already going to go through a lot of hay. That would be something to figure out tomorrow, when he had a full day to work.

Now he needed to get back to start cleaning as much of the barn out as he could. Once the barn stalls were clean, he could move the pile away from the back doors with the tractor and pile it in further back in the corral for later in the year. There had to be a manure spreader around somewhere. He would look for it tomorrow.

The barn was all cleaned out, with the Kid doing as much as he could in his first day. It was now time to go to the cookhouse. He had almost forgotten to call the cook to check in.

"Hey June got a copy, nothing? June, do you have a copy, nothing? Hey, Cookie, I have run out calf balls, need more. Do you have a copy?"

"Hey, Kid, sounds like you haven't lost your sense of humor. Did you like all the notes? Over!"

"Yeah, Cookie, the notes were great! I wonder how you were able to keep everything for so long, though. But you guys should have told me about the longhorns, over."

"Paul and I both thought he would surprise you with both bits of information, over."

"Is Paul there, over?"

"Kid, you're not going to get him to talk on the two-way radio. I finally just got him to answer the phone and then he just answers without saying anything. People just hang up, and that's all right by him! Kid, he is listening to what you're saying, over."

"June, thanks for cleaning out the cookhouse, over."

"Kid, the place was a mess. Couldn't let you move in with it like that! How do you like the place? Over."

"I am in flatlander paradise with all the food you brought me. Also, I finally have a bathroom, two to be exact! I think I'll take the one in the bedroom and give the one off the kitchen to Dawg, over."

"That got Paul's attention. What is the weather doing at the ranch? Over."

"It's fine. I really think you two are being a little bit too careful for the flatlander, although I wish there was a thermometer around, over."

"Kid, there is one right outside the kitchen window, over the counter, over."

"I see it, the thermometer says it's about eighteen below zero. That's not too bad, over."

"Kid, you should be glad you didn't let me cut your hair. You're probably going to need all the hair you have till winter is done, over."

"Yeah, I am going to look like the missing link when spring weather comes around. Paul and the dogs won't recognize me. Hey, when are my horses being brought over, over?"

"First chance they get. Everybody is getting ready for calving. Will call you for weather conditions, over."

"June, see if Paul would bring them over so I can show him the place, over."

"Kid, Paul says that would be fine. We should probably get back to what we're doing, and you remember to call, and I am serious about that now, over."

"Cookie, I will, and you folks have a good evening. Flatlander out."

The Kid finished his supper of a couple of cheeseburgers and chips. Now he was settling in with some homemade oatmeal raisin cookies and reading one of his Sackett books by the propane stove in his fully uptown bedroom. The Kid was as happy as he could remember ever being. He had Dawg, a good book, cookies, and milk by himself in paradise. Life was pretty good for the flatlander. He was enjoying the change so far.

During the next few days, he took the time to do an inventory of things that needed to be done. In that time, he found the only thing he had missed the first day was to make sure the bulls had open water for their drinking. After that, he packed a spud bar with him to break the ice if it needed it. But so far it looked like the water was open enough for the bulls to get a drink. It was just a little worry that would continue to nag at him throughout the long winter.

The next items on his inventory list were the rest of the ranch's buildings. He thought it would be good to be on familiar terms with all the different buildings or at least do a walkthrough making sure everything had been winterized.

There was a pretty big main house just inside the last gate as a person drives into the ranch; a bunkhouse with individual rooms for hired hands with a common area across from the horse barn; a building that looked to be a guest house for visitors; and a few old log cabins across from the cookhouse.

On the way to where the bulls were fed was one good-sized log building across from the little bridge. As he walked through the old building, he determined that it could have been used as a milking barn, thinking he would sure like to have fresh milk. Ever since he had access to his old dear, sweet Buttercup, he always liked a glass of warm, fresh milk.

In his travels, he also found what looked to be a bone pile of old, worn-out pieces of ranch equipment. He found there was a really old hay rack with runners on the bottom, a sleigh that would be good for hauling hay around feeding the bulls. He could pitch hay on the rack from the stack and then turn the horses lose pitching the hay off, similar to how he had learned to do at the first ranch with Walker. He could turn the horses loose like the John Deere tractor in low range. He thought, *Where are the horses going to go, and how fast can they run in all this snow?*

The sleigh was really old and probably should have been left in the bone pile, but all the important stuff was there. The Kid took the time to look over the sleigh, fixing some broken poles on the rack. The runners were in good shape, and the tongue, or reach as it is sometimes called, was in good shape also. Now he had to find the single and double trees (eveners) and the neck yoke to connect the horses to the reach. They surely were around somewhere.

It had taken the Kid a few afternoons to get the sleigh in working order. Now he was ready to harness the roan draft horses, seeing how well everything worked out. He had already made all the introductions and felt that maybe he was spoiled with the grays. The roan horses seem to take on a whole other set of personalities.

The Kid was just this slow, easygoing, big guy, and the roans seemed to have a real sense of excitement about them. All the Kid's animals had one common personality trait: they all were easygoing and deliberate about their motives. The roans just seemed to be fueled by emotion and not deliberate in any of their actions. Juicy or gassy is what the old cowboy called it.

Now the Kid wished he had the grays to do the test run with the sleigh. It might have a chance of staying together then. But the cook said Walker would be coming over in couple days with all three of the Kid's horses. Might as well find out what the roans were like hitched up. He might have some fun in the process.

In the corral, the Kid walked the roans around, trying to find out which position the horses worked in the hitch, gee or haw. Walker taught the Kid to look closely. All horses would eventually tell what he wanted to know.

Depending on who had worked the horses before, they could have a particular stall they were used to. Their harness could be hung on the peg next to that stall already fitted to the horse. All he had to do was look; the information was there.

He made his choice, tying the horses in a stall and going through the normal routine of brushing and checking the horses out. The Kid found it hard to believe the roans were taller than his grays. They were not as muscled up, though. That might come after they worked for awhile.

The Kid walked the roans out of the barn harnessed, looking over his work. He turned to Dawg, shrugging his shoulders. He hooked up the two horse lines to the bridles, and walking, he drove the roans to the sleigh.

The horses looked and felt like they wanted to do a little work walking into position on each side of the reach. He really had not expected the horses to be this easy to get along with. He hooked up the neck yoke's metal rings to the snaps on the breast strap and tracer chains to the single trees and climbed onto the sleigh.

Standing there behind the pole front of the sleigh, he gathered up the two horse lines, with his trusting Dawg beside him. Once he had the two horse lines even to the roans' bridles, he let a little bit of pressure off, giving the roans their heads. They hit their harness like horses on a mission. They made it out from the ranch buildings, over the little bridge, and past the old milking barn. Then, without much of a choice, he just turned the roans lose.

The horses took off out in the snow like they had a place to go and had to be there fast. The Kid and his always-trusting Dawg up to that point had not been on a runaway before—well, at least on a sleigh. The grays had never even showed the inclination of running away with the Kid. The only horses the Kid had been on in a runaway were the blacks, a pulling hitch the banker bought.

The ranch had enough draft horses for three hitches of four abreast, with some extra horses young and old alike to spare. The banker, having bought two horses out of a competition pulling hitch, thought the horses might make a good team for the ranch. But the banker quickly found out that the horses could not be trained not to pull like they were in a competition.

A wagon could be empty or loaded heavy, and those horses would pull hard. Once the horses broke the wagon from a standing still position, they were off and running. That is how they were taught from the beginning, to break hard and get to the finish winning.

The banker had even tried using trips on the horses, or what are also called Running W's. If the horses even started to break to run, a person is supposed to use a heavy cotton rope to pull on the horses' front legs, tripping them. The horses would get back up and you got to start the process over again, hopefully with the horse learning not to run. The horses really never quit breaking hard after all the work with the Running W's. They were taught to be winners.

The Kid had been the one pulling on the rope and had experienced horses running away then, but this was partly a different situation. He was on a sleigh with runners in snow and not on a wheeled wagon on dry ground. In fact, a tough ride.

Smiling, the Kid looked at his trusting Dawg as they were being pulled behind the horses, going like a bat out of hell. He decided to let the roans run all they wanted, with the sleigh gliding over the snow. The horses had already broken a trail, making the trip home relatively easy.

The Kid thought this combination would be a good way to break trail to a new stack. So he drove the roans to the current stack yard and then broke trail to the next full stack. The horses seemed to want to run some more. He decided to let them go into the deep snow, hopefully slowing them down. That's what he had done with the Roman nose-gray horse herding sheep that wanted to buck all the time. It made it harder for them to buck and easy to do what you want them to do. That is what Walker had taught him to do. After they started to walk again, he drove them back to breaking trail. He wondered if he was doing the right thing in letting the horses run. Walker had always said that once you let a team run, the horses always wanted to run like the competition horses. The Kid had not started the roans and wasn't sure that the horses were not already taught to run, same as the other horses in regard to pulling hard. Maybe if the Kid was to salt and pepper the horses with the grays, he could teach the roans to drive better. He would have to see when Walker came to drop off his horses and ask.

The Kid felt good at what he had accomplished in the last few days and looked forward to the old cowboy's visit. For now he needed to finish his day by checking the bulls' water and driving the roans back to the ranch to make his call to the cook.

"June, have you got a copy, over? June, have you got a copy, over?"

"Kid, I am all ears. How are things going for the flatlander from the Midwest, over?"

"I had a runaway with the roans today, over."

"Did everything turn out all right, over?"

"June, I fixed up an old sleigh to use in the snow, over."

"Yeah driving horses with a sleigh in snow isn't much harm. When I drove horses we almost never had enough snow on this side of the mountain, over."

"June, you used to drive horses, over?"

"Yeah, Kid, I am the one who taught Paul. Didn't he tell you about me teaching him, over?"

"No, he didn't, and I'll bet he is not by the radio either, over."

"Kid, you got me there. Paul is down at the calving shed looking after the heifers, over."

"Is he going to be able to bring my horses, over?"

"Yes, he figures he better do it now. The heifers will be starting to calf steady, and then he won't have the time. How is the road to the ranch, over?"

"June, it's blown in. There isn't a chance to drive the truck and trailer to the ranch. That's one reason I fixed up the sleigh, to drive the roans to the road. I'd like to see what Paul thinks about the roans and the sleigh, over."

"Kid, how about your horses? How are they going to get to the place, over?"

"June, I will put some hay on the sleigh. The horses should follow. If Paul has time, he can drive the roans back to the ranch. I can see if old Ugly will let me ride him bareback if he has the mind to, over."

"Kid, if you think that will work, I will tell Paul. What time do you want him at the main gate?"

"June, I get done feeding at around two in the afternoon. I'll drive the roans to the main gate after that, over."

"Kid, I will tell Paul to show up at about two thirty. But Paul probably will not have the time to stay like you both would want. At that time of day he has just a small window of time to get back here before it gets dark, over."

"I'd like to see you both if that were possible and maybe stay the night. I have plenty of food to go around, over."

"Kid I don't think my heart could take it, seeing you so happy. Besides, I would probably have to fight you both to get a chance to drive the roans, over."

"Yeah I had a lot of fun today, the runaway was a riot! I could not believe the roans had that much power, and really a person is at their mercy. It kind of reminded me of learning to ride old Ugly, over."

"Hey, Kid, remember how the hired man put that gag bit in Ugly's mouth, over?"

"Yeah, did he try to ride the old Ugly, over?"

"Kid, not only did he try to ride the old horse, he still believes the gag bit should work on old Ugly. The cowboy is still walking like he has been worked over by one of old Ugly's bad moods, over."

"Well doesn't that beat all? You should tell the cowboy Ugly won't let anyone sit in the saddle that he doesn't want on his back. That cowboy is a bad actor anyway and deserves what he gets, over!"

"Yeah, you sure like your animals. Kid, we had better stop talking. I make sure Paul gets all your information, over."

"Thanks, June, this is the flatlander out."

The Kid spent his first few days at the Hairpin without his favorite horses and was looking forward to sharing paradise with them when they got there. Additionally, he missed the cook and the old cowboy, wishing they all could be here to enjoy the good times. But the Kid was just going to have to settle spending the rest of the winter in paradise with all his animals.

After feeding the bulls, the Kid drove the roans to the main road to meet Walker. In recent memory, he could not remember when he last was so excited to see someone. As he rounded the corner, there at the end of road past the main gate was the truck and trailer already waiting.

There the banker's yellow truck was running, with the old cowboy sitting on the seat, smiling at seeing the Kid driving the roans. All the Kid's horses were tied to the outside of the trailer, with all heads turned in the direction of the sleigh. After seeing all his friends watching, the Kid got a little nervous and gathered up his two horse lines, with the roans feeling the tension on their bits. Before the Kid knew it, the roans were off and running.

Chewing his tobacco, the old cowboy got out of truck to watch the show, smiling from ear to ear. Ugly, Rocky, and Lucky now were all nickering at seeing their young friend fast coming in their direction. The sleigh with the Kid and his always trusting Dawg were flying through the snow, with hopes they could keep from going to town for a day off.

When approaching the main gate at a pretty good clip, the Kid decided to drift the roans into the field, slowing the runaway broncos down for just a bit more control. The Kid got the horses walking about the time they were at the main gate, swinging them around to a stop just short of the truck and trailer.

"Kid, looks like you got things under control."

Smiling, the Kid dropped the inside tracer chains on the roans and looped his lines around the rack on the sleigh.

"Paul, how was your trip over?"

"Kid, this old rig can make for some good time. The banker has the truck so juiced up; the rig could probably win a pulling contest against your grays."

"I'd like to see that contest! But what I'd like to see is a race between the roans and the banker's yellow rig. They just seem to want to run all the time. The roans remind me of the pulling horses that we put the trips on. Paul, do you know anything about these runaway roans?"

"Kid, I know the history of most of the animals around the territory. All the natives around the territory know what cowboy has worked what horse and how the horse turned out. Just like they know you are here by yourself with your horses for the winter.

"But now I think it is time for you to figure the roans out for yourself. After all your good work with the gray horses that I brought you today, I think if you use some of that horse sense they taught. You should do just fine."

"Paul, it sounds like you're weaning me."

"It has to happen sometime in a Kid's life. Besides, I would like to see what you can do by yourself. You have to develop some of your own ways of getting the animals to do what you need them to do. I have given you some of my fundamentals; now use them to get you to where you want to go."

"You're cutting me off. That could be tough on a lot of things."

"Kid, I think the world of you and what you have already done with the animals you see here. I'm not going to be around forever. I would like to see how you use my information. I want to see how much further you can take it, if you can."

"Paul, everything all right? You seem a little off."

"Yeah, I'm fine. Now June had me bring you some more groceries."

The two friends unloaded the goodies, talking just a little while more. They said their good-byes, and Walker drove off, spinning his wheels in the snow.

There the Kid stood next to the sleigh with Dawg, and all his horses were tied to the sleigh or hitched to it. He first said his hello to Ugly and then the grays. Dawg gave all the horses his greeting of smelling noses, especially Ugly. All concerned were happy to be back together again.

The Kid hooked up the inside tracers to the roans, gathered up his two horse lines, and drove the sleigh to the inside of the main gate. Once there, he used his feet to clear as much snow as needed to shut the gates behind him.

Then he thought that if Walker was turning him loose, he should do the same to Ugly and the grays, and he turned each horse lose. Then with Dawg, he climbed back on the sleigh, gathering up his two horse lines and giving the roans their heads.

Now the roan horses were running through the snow at below zero temperatures with him and his trusting Dawg on the sleigh. At the same time, the grays were running on different sides of the sleigh, shaking their heads and kicking at the air with their black harnesses flapping. Old Ugly was out front, running down the trail the Kid had made coming out. The Kid had never felt more alive and at ease with his life. He has to be in paradise now that all his friends were with him.

The race continued toward the ranch buildings, eventually slowing to a walk. The Kid drove the roans through the last gate to a particular spot where he wanted to stop the sleigh. There were a couple of poles on the ground he had to stop the front and back runners on. He found that at cold temperatures, the runners froze down to the ground, making it difficult for the horses to start a load. The poles kept the runners from freezing down.

Climbing down to unhook the tracers, all the horses were checking each other out, with Dawg staying on the sleigh. After taking the bridles and lines off the Roans, hanging them on the respective horses' harnesses, the Kid walked the roans in the barn.

There the roans were eating hay, with the Kid doing his normal routine of checking them out from their day of work. All the while, the grays had their big heads looking through the barn door, checking out their new home. Ugly was eating hay off the sleigh, with Dawg helping by eating any mice that might get in the way. Now it was time to say hello to his old friends.

The Kid led the grays to their stalls for oats and hay. After hanging up the harnesses on pegs outside their stalls and then wiping down the collars from all the sweat, he looked over the horses for any problems that might have happened in the time he hadn't been around them.

He thought maybe there might be some galling on Rocky's shoulders and would wait, looking again in the morning. Once the horses had cooled down after spending the night, the cold temperatures would show warm spots where the galling happened. Just to make sure, the Kid decided he would use the treatment saltwater to toughen up both grays' shoulders. They were going to be working every day now. It was better safe than sorry later down the road.

While the grays were eating hay from their mangers, he rubbed them down with straw. Then he took a curry comb from the front of the forelock to the tip of their tail and combed them out. Lucky always stood still and just ate, but Rocky always liked to lean on his Kid, pinning him against the stall partition. Once pinned, the old horse liked to use his lips to pull at his Kid's clothes, pinching wherever he could. The Kid always liked all the attention Rocky was willing to show from always being in the good mood to play.

The grays were finished, and now it was Ugly's turn for some attention. Looking at his friends, the Kid took a moment to watch the horse and Dawg. The two were old buddies, and it was something to see how they are so at ease with each other. Ugly was eating his hay, standing lose in his stall, and Dawg was lying right behind the old war pony's back hooves, asleep, of all things.

Stepping easy around Dawg, he said his hello to Ugly. The horse took the time from eating to give his Kid a nudge with his nose. The Kid worked on Ugly, feeling a sense of peace, that this was what he was intended to do, at least for the time being, hanging out and taking care of all his good friends in paradise.

Letting the horses finish their hay, he tried to figure the best way to give the horses as much room to get around as possible. He decided for now to keep the roans with the little bay where they had been in the corral. After the roans and little bay were corralled, he could just let the rest lose and couldn't imagine the horses not coming to him. They would have access to feed and water. He just liked the idea of the horses having as much freedom as he could give them. It went back to how Walker had treated his horses at cow camp. He would work on the roans and the little bay till he could catch them. Then they could have as much room to get around as the others.

The horses were done eating, and the sun was going down, with the temperature turning colder. The Kid had the best of days, and it was time to call the cook.

"Hey, Cookie, you have a copy? Over."

"Yeah, Kid, I am here, over."

"Boy, you are right by the radio this time, over."

"Did Paul make it all right with your horses and goodies, over?"

"June, Paul made it here just fine, and he should be showing up anytime your way, over."

"Thanks, Kid. How was your visit, and did your horses recognize you, over?"

"Sure the horses recognized me. It's like old times. I am looking forward to using the grays tomorrow. I bet old Ugly will follow just to hang out with Dawg, over."

"Where are you keeping your horses that you can just let the Ugly run loose, over?"

"June, there is a field just off from the ranch buildings that I turned them loose in. I left the gate open to the ranch buildings from the field so they can come and go to get feed and water, over."

"Kid, you going to be able to catch the horses, over?"

"Yeah, I got all the water and feed right here. Besides, the snow is deep everywhere else. June, I think I have been weaned, over."

"Kid, you have been what, over?"

"Paul said that he gave me my start on working with horses and that I needed to take it from here, over."

"Kid, then it is good you are all by yourself so you are the only one who gets hurt. It's probably going to help that you're in the Big Hole where there is a lot of snow. It will help break your fall a little. You better wear as much padding as you can get on, over."

"Well aren't you just the ornery one today? Paul cuts me off like a cow weaning its starving calf and you make jokes about it, over."

"Kid, here is another point that should be made. Paul was the last visitor you going to see for quite a while, over."

"Now you are just messing with me! Sounds like we need another fishing contest, maybe here at the Hairpin. One I can win this time using bullheads for bait. That will give me all the time I need to tell all the fish here what happened the last time we had a contest and how many of their relatives you killed in what had to be the biggest carnage of fish I have ever seen, over."

"Kid, we can have it anywhere you want. But you better buy a good knife and have it sharp, because you're going to be cleaning all the fish like last time, over."

"Yeah, I hear you, Cookie! But this time you cannot take all the bullheads, leaving me catching grasshoppers for bait, over."

"Kid, grasshoppers are good bait, over."

"Cookie, I don't think that's the point! I was trying to catch the little flying hoppers while you were fishing. Once I figured out what you had done with all the bait, grasshoppers were the only other choice to use as bait. I was flat on my stomach crawling on the ground, sneaking up on grasshoppers all the time you were pulling fish out the creek like a person on a mission, over."

"I was on a mission! I couldn't let a flatlander beat me at fishing could I, over?"

"June, I spent most of the day cleaning your fish. I think it could be said you cheated, over."

"Kid, here on the ranch the natives call that educating the tourists, over."

"No longer am I a flatlander. Are you calling me a tourist now, over?"

"Hey, Kid, how cold is it getting over there, over?"

"You're trying to change the subject. It's not bad at all, maybe ten below zero. Why, over?"

"I think it's time I should tell you Paul's secret to staying warm, over."

"Sure, June, if it gets cold like everybody is telling me, I could use all the tips that I can get, over."

"Kid this is going to be a shock, so you better have a seat, over!"

"What are you up to now, Cookie, over?"

"When it gets really cold, under his long johns Paul wears pantyhose, over!"

"Cookie, I don't think you should have told me that. Surely Paul wouldn't want you to broadcast it over the radio for everyone who is listening, over!"

"Kid, do you think all those cowboy heroes in your books wore pantyhose, over?"

"Now you are just being mean. This has to be your biggest FLN joke yet. Cookie, you are never going to make me believe Paul wears pantyhose, over."

"Kid, you better wait till it gets fifty or sixty below zero and then tell me that, over."

"June, I guarantee no matter how cold it gets, I am never going to wear pantyhose, over."

"Well, I just thought that it would be a good idea to send you some anyway. There is a pair in the bag of goodies I sent for you. I hope they fit. It was extremely hard to find something in your size, over."

"Yeah, yeah! June, have you been drinking or working too many days straight? Maybe need a little time off. Maybe you should try some of Paul's chewing tobacco, over."

"Kid, Paul just pulled in with the truck and trailer. I had better get him something ready to eat, over."

"Yeah, you better sign off! Paul isn't going to like everybody knowing that he wears women's undergarments. I better do the same, over."

The Kid sat the mike on its stand, staring at the bag of goodies sitting on the kitchen counter. He really did not want to know that pantyhose were in that bag of goodies. The FLN cook had played a lot of jokes on the Kid since their first days on the ranch, like internal organs in the pantry, for instance.

He looked from the bag of goodies to his ever-trusting Dawg, thinking maybe Dawg should look first in the big bag of goodies. Dawg promptly sat, turning his head from side to side looking innocent, his default position in circumstances like this.

The Kid really needed to unpack the bag, seeing all the good stuff the cook had sent. There could be all kinds of cookies, candy, and snacks. But there was a high risk that loomed in the bag of goodies, a pair of women's undergarments. There was always a real possibility the FLN cook had put them there.

Laughing almost at the point of tears, the Kid looked into the bag, finding a huge batch of peanut butter cookies in a big zip bag. Ooh those are good. Next he found a plate of dark chocolate fudge bars. Oh, those are good too. Then there is and always are fresh veggies, lettuce, tomatoes, and bacon for BLT sandwiches. Umm, those are good. Then as he took the veggies out from the bottom of the bag, to his horror were his pantyhose. Were there no limits to the FLN cook's humor?

He took the pantyhose out of the bag, reading the label to Dawg. "Change your figure with the double elastic band." Laughing, the Kid very gently laid the pantyhose on the table, thinking, heck he had never even seen a pair this close before. How else are you supposed to set pantyhose on the table? Pausing, he decided to cover them with an old newspaper, out of sight out of mind.

After eating his BLT sandwich and cookies, he went to bed, laughing at all the rough and tough hired hands at the main ranch taking their woman's undergarments off before going to bed.

The next day, the Kid woke at his normal time, 5:00 a.m. After turning on the kitchen lights, he was somewhat startled to find Rocky looking through the front door window, making nose prints. The Kid looked through the window, saying good morning as Rocky blew air from his nose, making the window fog up.

After fixing his breakfast of scrambled eggs, he sat at the table to eat. There was that package from last night, as he decided to call it now, covered with the newspaper. He slid it down the table far enough away that it was not in his field of vision. Outside in the dark, Rocky, of course, was looking through the kitchen windows, watching the Kid eat his food, wondering what was taking so long. He had oats on his mind.

Just as the Kid and Dawg cracked open the front door, their nosey neighbor was there to help in the difficult process of the grand opening. Dawg took off for places unknown, with the Kid trying one of those quick movie jumps onto the back of the horse a couple of times. Maybe he should just walk.

The Kid walked towards the barn, with Rocky pinching at his coat and gloves with his lips. "Hey there, Rocky, where is the rest of your band of outlaws?" Smiling, Rocky's Kid opened the barn to have the old gray going to each stall, checking for leftover oats. After the Kid put oats in all the feed boxes, it was now time to check out Rocky's shoulders for galling.

As Rocky ate his oats, the Kid gave the gray a good brushing. At the same time, the Kid was taking a close look at anything that might look out of sorts, like warms spots on the shoulders where the collar rubbed, galling.

Once he was satisfied, the Kid put Rocky's collar over his head down to his shoulders. Once there, his Kid checked the spacing between the bottom of the horse's neck and collar using his fingers; it was good.

The next step was where the Kid could take advantage of his height. The harness was hanging on a high peg beside the back of the gray's stall. He used his left hand to lift the breeching off the peg and on to his right arm till the hames were in each hand, heavy. He carried the harness the short distance to the gray's back, keeping the hames separated to fit around the gray's collar. As the breeching laid on the gray's back, he aligned the hames to fit in the collar's front edge, using the hames' silver tops as his gauge for even and buckled the hames in place, using the hames strap.

Next he let the breeching fall into place on each side of the gray, picking up the tail so the breeching could go into place on his back legs. The harness didn't have a crupper for the tail. From here the two quarter straps were snapped to the ring of the pole strap, and last, the belly band got buckled.

By the time he had Rocky all lined out for his work day, the rest of the outlaws were walking in the barn to their respective stalls getting their oats, and the Kid harnessed Lucky for his day's work.

The Kid was excited to hitch up the grays to see if they're that much better than the roans. The two horse lines to the grays' bridles were snapped in place, and the Kid drove them out the barn door as the morning sun started to come up over the ridges.

Driving the grays to the sleigh, the horses, with confidence, stepped over the reach in place all squared up. They knew their job and were just anxious to be back working with their Kid. Next the Kid put the end of each neck yoke through each gray's pole strap, snapping the breast strap to the metal rings on the neck yoke.

With the two horse lines over his right shoulder, he stepped behind each horse, attaching the set of trace chains to the single trees on the double tree.

The Kid now took a little time to check anything that might look out of sorts—a bottom hames strap might need tightening, a quarter strap might need adjusting, making sure each tracer chain was the same amount of links off the trace; so far so good.

The Kid took the big step to get up on the sleigh where Dawg was already waiting. Smiling, he gathered up his lines between his fingers, making sure all was even going to the grays' bridles. The grays took notice, squaring to each other, waiting for their Kid to take a little pressure off the bits. That told them it was time to go to work.

He took his last look to make sure the hames' silver tops were even and that the grays were leaning into their harness even to each other, taking any slack out of the trace chains. The double tree was even.

Dawg and Ugly were waiting patiently for the start of their day with their Kid, knowing he was just a little fussy about the grays.

As the Kid gave the grays their heads, both leaned into their collars, taking their first step in unison, moving the sleigh off the poles. Smiling and shaking his head, the Kid looked on in amazement at the sight of the horses working together. Not only were they a matched set in looks, but they made the Kid look so good at how easy they were to drive and work. In this scenario, they were the teachers and the Kid was the student.

The Kid stood on the sleigh, looking around at all the critters that were a part of this day. Dawg was out front leading the way, and following close behind was Ugly with head up, looking around at his new home in the Big Hole Valley. Following was the Kid driving the grays in what had to be the most beautiful place on earth.

They were all working at an elevation of about sixty-three hundred feet, with snow-covered mountains close in the background. The ranch was at the foothills of these mountains, covered in a blanket of deep snow that had everything gleaming in sparkling crystals from the sun rising over the snow-covered peaks.

If not for the area the Kid used for feeding, the snow would not have a mark or print showing anything lived there. The only noise the Kid could hear was the runners scraping on the snow. There was not any other evidence that there was any other human being on the place except for him. Now the Midwest flatlander Kid had his answer; everything at the Hairpin was the best now that he had all of his friends with him. He was one happy young man.

Tracks

The Kid and his animals had been at the Hairpin for a couple months. He met an adversary in the Big Hole Valley that cared little that he was big as a bear and hard headed—Old Mother Nature. He had only survived by figuring out little details that made it possible for him to cope with the well below-zero temperatures. There had been only a couple of occasions she had made the Kid almost say he had had enough, with temperatures going to more than forty below zero.

It should be said this number was without the wind-chill factor, and of course, his thermometer only went to forty below. He had thought on numerous occasions that he would have liked to know what the actual temperatures were, if for nothing else than for the fun of the bragging rights. But he found out really fast that maybe it was best not to brag till winter was over. His adversary, Old Mother Nature, might not like the fact of someone boasting about something she took a lot of pride in doing.

To think after just a short time in the Big Hole Valley, he had the audacity to believe that he had survived all of her harshest weather conditions. Old Mother Nature laughed at the Midwest flatlander Kid, because she still had plenty left in her bag of tricks. She had weeks of colder temperatures, snow drifts at unbelievable heights, the sun's reflection off the white snow that made sunglasses a necessity, winds of what had to be up to thirty miles an hour, and snowing and blowing so hard that the Kid could hardly see the grays pulling the sleigh.

The Kid had laughed on numerous occasions when it got to snowing and blowing so hard. He thought the snow was just from the neighbors miles down the road and not from new snow falling. The old girl, Mother Nature, was just recycling her snow on the ground, saving the new stuff for a different time.

He remembered the conversations he had with the old cowboy and the cook cautioning him on how different the temperatures were in the Big Hole Valley compared to the main ranch. It was colder. But until now, after four years of ranching, he had not found any problems with the normal day-to-day weather conditions that Old Mother Nature had thrown at him, a flatlander. Well maybe except for what had to be a storm cloud of those little buzzing insects, mosquitoes. He hated those little buzzing insects.

On those times of weakness, the Kid took notice of how all the animals, his friends, seemed to pick his spirits up. They just made the Kid smile at how blessed he was being together with such good friends. All the circumstances that had brought them all together and the affection they all had come to find for each other was remarkable.

Rocky would be at the kitchen windows every morning trying to get a look at his Kid inside despite the cold temperatures. The old gray would go from window to window, making nose prints and fogging the window glass with his breath. Rocky just wanted to see what his Kid was doing that took him so long to come out. He really needed his oats and wanted his Kid to hurry up.

Ugly never seemed to stop amazing the Kid with his attachment to Dawg. The old war pony, in all the battles fought with cowboys in the rodeo, showed remarkable sensitivity to all his friends. Dawg just seemed to be his favorite.

The roans and little bay were starting to become a part of the Kid's family of friends also. The horses seemed to like the new freedom of roaming around that the Kid started when he arrived at the ranch. The horses were still a little standoffish but were coming around. The Kid would wait, letting the other horses bring them into his way of doing things. Once the whole bunch had developed into a family, the Kid would try to see if he could take the edge off the roans.

The horse that was the key to making it all work was Lucky. From what the Kid had been told, the grays had been together since the first time they had harness put on their backs. The two were as close to being matched in looks as any two horses the Kid had ever seen. The differences were in their personalities.

Rocky was this lovable character that always was finding ways of pestering his Kid to get more oats. Sometimes the Kid would tease the old horse, taking his good old time walking to the barn in the morning. Rocky used his nose to tug at his clothes, looking in all his pockets in hopes of finding some oats and to get him to move along a little faster. The Kid finally climbed on his back, and the old gray gave him a ride the rest of the way to his first of what had to be many by this time portions of oats.

But Lucky was the boss of the two and actually should be said the only adult of the whole bunch of outlaws. The gray was stronger through the chest and more alert to what was happening around him.

Lucky was always ready for work and always the first to lean into his harness to start a load, with the Rocky but a fraction of time behind. They both would get to their knees to pull if the weight of the load required them to. Lucky was always the first to recognize a heavy load, and Rocky could be thinking of anything other than work, maybe oats. Rocky only noticed these important things once Lucky started to point them out.

When Rocky got Lucky irritated for his playing around all the time, once in awhile he had to impose discipline by biting Rocky. Then Rocky was obedient till he found the next thing to distract him from all that Lucky needed him to do.

The Kid loved the Rock for his good nature, but he knew Lucky was the horse that made the hitch work. If the team had two horses like Rocky, a person would not get a whole lot of work accomplished, although you would have a lot of fun and probably run out of oats pretty quick.

To make the Kid smile on those really cold days, Dawg had even submitted to wearing the pantyhose moccasins his Kid had made for him special, even though all the other animals would laugh at him wearing woman's undergarments. Dawg's friend had to find a way to keep his paws from freezing to the snow at the really cold temperatures, and it was also better that Dawg wear the damn undergarment than him. Dawg just stood by, letting his friend fit what had to be the worst-looking set of moccasins a Dawg could wear; fortunately for him, all his dog friends were at the main ranch.

While wearing his custom-fitted moccasins, Dawg kept trying to mess with the longhorns, continuing to get banged up; the Kid loved that about Dawg. Even though he knew or had to know by now he did not have a chance against the bulls, he continued to try to help his Kid out. Dawg has always somehow found something to do that made his Kid smile.

The temperatures now were hovering just over the zero mark, and it felt to the Kid like spring. He even had to take his flap-in-the back red long johns off and at times wore his cowboy hat to work in.

He was not getting too excited about the change in weather. Winter or at least snow would be on the ground in the Big Hole Valley till probably late April and probably a little into May. He wasn't kidding himself that spring is just around the corner.

Since the balmy weather had arrived, colder temperature chores were wait and see, breaking ice for the bulls' drinking water, for one. He had a little more time now to check some things out that had been bothering him most of the winter.

There were tracks that had been showing up in different places that he had not had the time to check out. The tracks showed up mostly at night, and it was hard with all the deep snow to identify what was making them.

The one set of tracks he was curious about went to and from the pile of whatever was outside the back door of the cookhouse. The pile was maybe fifty to seventy feet away from the back door and appeared to be just snow. There had to be something in the pile the little critters wanted.

So the Kid got the tractor, Dawg and Rocky to follow close behind, the sheriff and his deputies. The other horses, the smart ones, had seen these three get into similar situations before when bored. They were going to stay as far away as possible from what was surely going to be trouble in the making.

Even old Ugly had watched his good friend Dawg turn his head, giving him that look of, "Oh come on, this will be fun." The old war pony that had and still could buck off everything that tried to ride him walked the other way, as if saying, "You guys are always getting into trouble." The sheriff and his deputies always seemed to find something of interest to stir up a little fun, and the old bucker just wanted to watch from a safe distance this time.

The posse was looking over the tracks, all walking in a line of who could get in the most trouble first. The tracks went from the pile back of the cookhouse to underneath one of the really old log cabins quite a distance away.

The sheriff had really never paid any attention to smaller tracks before. He wanted to learn how to hunt an elk or maybe a deer and would need to identify those tracks. The smaller ones really were of no interest to him till now. It was just something to do. The sheriff spent a little time bent down looking at the tracks with deputies Dawg and Rocky by his side doing the same. All with lowered heads were either looking or using their noses, trying to somehow extract scent from what outlaw had made these tracks.

The sheriff would move a foot or two, stop, and then point to the tracks, showing his two deputies the evidence. Dawg would stick his nose down, smelling the tracks the sheriff was pointing out. Rocky kept sticking his nose into the sheriff's pockets, looking for oats that were his for the taking. He knew the sheriff had put the oats there to bribe him to be a part of the posse. He just had to find the right pocket.

The sheriff decided to slowly follow the tracks with deputy Dawg already out front, looking under the old cabin for the would-be outlaws. Deputy Rocky, staying with the sheriff, took great delight in nudging the Kid over with his nose every time he would bend down to look over any of the tracks. He just had to have some oats. Maybe they were in a different pocket. The Kid would get up from the snow, telling deputy Rocky he had better quit or else. Deputy Rocky would nudge him over again, seemingly to smile every time the sheriff had to get back up.

Shaking his head laughing, the sheriff finally gave up trying to identify the tracks and walked back to the tractor, leaving the two deputies to themselves. The sheriff at least wanted to find out for one what in tarnation was in the pile of whatever that has grabbed the attention of whatever belongs to those tracks. Surely what's in the pile would be a clue and maybe enough information to identify the band of outlaws.

The pile looked to be so out of the sorts from everything else. It had to be more than just snow. It had not taken the sheriff long to get his answer. Under about three feet of snow was trash, bags and bags of trash.

The sheriff remembered the note about the condition that the cookhouse was in when the cook had cleaned it out. There was no way the cook would have cleaned up this much trash. It had to be the folks who had been fired. The sheriff thought, *Why in the world would anybody just throw bags of trash out their back door?* Now what was he going to do with all this trash?

The sheriff sat on the tractor, contemplating the issue, when the deputy Dawg ran past the tractor with deputy Rocky close on his heels. The sheriff had a bewildered look on his face watching his two deputies very quickly go by and then the smell hit him—outlaws.

The sheriff looked over his shoulder and saw two skunks in that tail-pointing-to-the-sky posture. Now in a little bit of a hurry, when he tried to put the tractor in gear, he popped the clutch. Shit, he hadn't done that in a long time. The smelly outlaws were now running toward the tractor, with the sheriff making his fast getaway, grinding gears.

The posse was going as fast as they could, with the smelly outlaws chasing close behind with guns pointing to the sky, ready to take a smelly shot.

Hearing all the commotion, the rest of the horses popped their heads up, looking in the direction of the getaway. The sheriff was driving the tractor, with the deputies running through all the ranch buildings, with the smelly outlaws close on their tail! As horses will do, they stopped what they were doing and joined the runaway posse out across the small bridge, past the old milking barn, and into the field behind the ranch buildings.

Once the sheriff thought that he was at a safe distance, he stopped and turned the tractor to face the ranch buildings. All the horses kept running past him, jumping and kicking their feet. The sheriff looked in the direction they had come to see, in horror, the outlaw skunks pacing back and forth on the bridge with tails ready for anything that came back their way. The sheriff could only assume that the outlaw skunks had taken over the town of Hairpin.

The deputy Dawg and the horses were soon gathered around the tractor—well, sort of. It seemed that the deputies were to themselves, away from the rest. The Kid looked to the ranch buildings, making sure the outlaw skunks were still protecting the town of Hairpin. Yes!

He got off the tractor and walked over to check out his two deputies. Deputy Dawg started rolling back and forth in the snow, rubbing his face, and Deputy Rocky just looked at the sheriff hoping for some sympathy. The two deputies were hit in their faces with smelly bullets. They tried to get help from the sheriff, and he just circled the tractor, keeping at least that amount of distance between him and their new animal fragrance.

There the sheriff stood on one side off the tractor with all the grownups and the deputies Dawg and Rocky on the other side, waiting for the smelly outlaws to leave there strategic position of the bridge.

"Hey, Cookie, you got your ears on, over?"

"Yeah, Kid, there you go again with the CB radio lingo. You must be having a good day, over."

"Yeah, I have had a good day, and I need another piece of advice, over."

"OK, Kid, what did you and those animals of yours do now, over?"

"Cookie, we had a band of outlaw skunks that thought they were tough enough to run us out of the Hairpin. Just now were able to retake the town, over!"

"Kid, it's your band of outlaws that has you in all these situations, not the stripped ones! Did you get sprayed, over?"

"Not me, it is Dawg and Rocky that got sprayed in the face, over."

"I can understand Dawg. But how in the world did the gray get sprayed, over?"

The Kid told the cook his story and asked for advice in how to neutralize the skunk smell on his two deputies.

"Kid, what in the world are you going to do with all that trash, over?"

"I think there are some old fifty gallon barrels I can use to burn the trash in, over."

"Well then you can try tomato paste, lemon juice, or anything that has acidity in it to help with the smell, over."

"The acidity neutralizes the smell, over?"

"Yes it will, but it sounds like when the warmer temperatures hit, you guys just could not stay out of trouble, over."

"I am certainly glad for the warmer temperatures. Now I can take time to have a little fun checking some things that have been nagging at me, like this pile of trash, over."

"Kid, you always liked to put things in order, and Paul wants to know if you have had the chance to check out the other tracks, over."

"Yeah the set of tracks out front of the ranch are from a cow moose and her calf. I saw the tracks when Paul brought the horses over a while back. I had just the time to go that way when the temperatures started coming up. I guess the cow moose and her calf have been there for awhile, probably eating willows and whatever else they can find, over."

"That is a ways to walk. Did you try to ride Ugly, over?"

"Yes I did. I thought it would be nice to take a ride on the old war pony, over."

"Kid, did he try to buck you off, over?"

"Cookie, me and that old war pony are good friends. He got a little humpy just to show me he is still boss, and I was glad to have a little excitement, over."

"Paul wants to know if the rest of the animals went on the trip, over."

"Like always, Dawg and Rocky just had to follow, and the rest figured out it is probably safer for them to stay at home, over."

"Kid, Paul wants to know if you are still letting the horses run around like at cow camp, over."

"Yeah, at first the horses thought they were escaping from being in the corral. But now that they have had the chance to run around free, pretty much getting to do what they want, they just hang out in the corral and eat hay. In the morning, Rocky, as always, comes to give me a ride to the barn, over."

"Kid, one last thing and I got to go do some cooking. Paul wants you to check out the other tracks that come out of the mountains, over."

"June, tell Paul that is next on the list for me, over."

"OK, Kid, tell us what you find out and we will talk at you later, over."

"You bet, and thanks for the help, over."

Now he had to look for something that would neutralize the skunk smell. The pantry was full of a lot of tomato paste and sauce, but in the winter? The thought had crossed his mind at how funny both deputies would look all covered in red tomato paste. He smiled to himself. What he did find was some condensed lime juice in a little green lime-like container. He remembered seeing an old empty spray bottle of something or another and cleaned it out.

He looked out the kitchen window, and the deputies seemed to be waiting for their treatment of watered-down lime juice in a spray bottle. The Kid opened the kitchen door to a smell that would gag a person of a strong constitution; the smell made the Kid wince. The deputies, of course, wanted to get close and rub all over their Kid. He stepped back with his lime squirt gun and sprayed his stinky deputies with his only weapon, watered down condensed lime juice in a spray bottle.

After spraying deputy Dawg first, he had to go get a refill to spray down deputy Rocky. Then he took a bath towel and wiped the two as dry as he could because of the cold temperatures. The Kid shook his head, hoping the lime juice worked, and threw the bath towel in the burning trash barrels.

Now Rocky would stay outside, as always. What would he do with Dawg? The temperatures were above zero, and he decided he would leave the two deputies to stay outside together. The Kid went into the cookhouse, leaving them standing at the door, looking pretty miserable.

Going about his evening, he tried to set aside the thought of Dawg outside all night by himself. After the few years he had Dawg, he had yet to spend any time away from the lunatic animal. He ate his supper of spaghetti and meat sauce with sautéed mushrooms, all the while thinking he should check on Dawg and make sure he was all right.

It took him almost till bedtime to go outside and have a look. He carried some of his leftover spaghetti in a bowl and looked for Dawg. The Kid was getting a little nervous that maybe he should have let Dawg stay in the cookhouse for the night and had one other place to look: the open barn. There in the barn aisle was Dawg, all curled up next to the old war pony, Ugly. They both lifted their heads and looked at the Kid as if to say, "There is room for one more!"

The Kid, holding his nose, stood shaking his head at the two friends and set the bowl of spaghetti down for Dawg. He then took the short walk up to the loft and picked up a bale of straw for their bedding. After the Kid spread the straw out for Dawg and his friend Ugly, he picked up the empty bowl and walked back to cookhouse to bed, leaving Dawg and Ugly to their dreams of chasing skunks and bucking cowboys off.

The Kid woke up to Rocky and Dawg looking in one of the kitchen windows. He checked the temperature and logged it down—fifteen above! He felt a little better about leaving Dawg outside last night. Now he needed to breach the smell barrier of the cookhouse and harness the horses. He went outside to the same awful smell, but it was not as bad. The lime juice had worked some, and he would apply another application again after feeding.

Today with the warmer temperatures, the Kid would have the time to check on the other set of tracks that were coming out of the mountains to his stack yard. The tracks had started showing up around the stack yard when Old Mother Nature's temperatures were well below zero.

At that time, the Kid tried to look at the tracks and thought his horses had made the tracks. Now he wasn't so sure because more and more it was just him, Dawg, and the grays feeding. The rest of the horses seemed to have gotten over all the excitement of going along. The tracks that the grays made were easy to distinguish and follow. These tracks were coming out from different places in the direction of the foothills of the mountains away from the ranch. He wished he had a spotting scope to scan the tree lines of the mountains.

There were only a couple choices for the Kid to make. He could follow the tracks to see where they went. That was next to impossible. The snow was deep, and Walker had told him about trying to see an animal following tracks. It was not going to happen, because you were always behind it. The other choice was waiting till the animal came back to the haystack after dark. The

Kid liked the idea of sleeping in his sleeping bag on top of the haystack under stars waiting for whatever would come—an adventure!

He would make his call to the cook, eat a little supper, and then take Dawg, the old cowboy's Winchester, and some jerky to spend the night. If he was fortunate, the moon would be almost full or full and he would have enough light from the reflection off the snow to see. He and Dawg would climb to the top of the haystack and be relatively safe from anything on the ground.

The thing that was bothering him was how to get there. The Kid thought about riding Ugly and just turning him lose after, but the old war pony would stay with Dawg at the haystack. Finally, the Kid made the decision to walk the distance. He had the lunatic Dawg by his side, and what animal would try to do anything with the threat of the skunk-smelling deputy by his side?

Then of course he had Walker's Winchester that he had used to take a couple of practice shots at the outlaw skunks after they still wanted to fight over town ownership. He had started to take the Winchester with him feeding when the coyotes started to get after Dawg. The timing of him starting to carry the Winchester and the outlaw skunks still wanting to finish any scraps of trash in the pile made for a bad set of circumstances.

The flatlander sharpshooter basically had taken aim with the Winchester as the outlaw skunks were trying to escape, running around the corner of the cookhouse. He did everything right, steadied the barrel of the Winchester, held his breath, and squeezed the trigger, and well … the sharpshooter hit the bottom corner of the cookhouse, twice if once wasn't good enough. The Kid smiled that nervous look and thought, *Shit, that ought to teach the outlaw skunks a lesson, killing the recently refurbished cookhouse!*

But he did remember the Winchester had a pretty good kick and if nothing else would scare anything away from the cannonlike noise it made. Between having the smelly Dawg and the noisy Winchester, he had enough protection to sleep waiting for the mystery animal.

As the Kid worked feeding the bulls, his eyes were watering from the smell of yesterday's fight with smelly outlaws. He had to work around the deputies that were sprayed in the dispute over ownership of trash. The Kid finally had to cover his face with his silk bandana and hope the wind would blow in a different direction.

As the day progressed, he took notice of all signs that might give any clue as to what the animal was and if it had been at the stack anytime recently. He saw tracks that were somewhat blown over by the wind and filled with snow. This gave him the direction the animal came from, which to some extent he already knew. All the other evidence was in the stack yard mixed with all the other tracks that were there from the grays. The Kid looked around the whole stack yard like he knew what he was doing but did not find anything that would give away a clue as to what the animal was.

Once he fed the bulls their loads of hay and had checked the water for ice, he decided to drive the grays as far as he could with an almost empty sleigh following the old tracks. The snow was a few feet deep and had a little crust on top from the warmer temperatures. He drove the grays to the base of the foothills to have a look around.

The sleigh was an easy pull from being close to empty, and if it were not for the deep snow, the Kid would have gone farther. As the Kid let the horses blow and catch their breath, he wondered what in the world could be trying to survive in all this snow. The animal was surviving the winter in all the Big Hole snow and cold by itself. The Kid thought this was a good spot for the hay and started to make a little trail of hay back in the direction of the stack yard, lasting for only about thirty feet. Then the Kid drove the grays to the haystack and loaded the sleigh for the next day.

Finishing with his chores, he prepared for the night's adventure. He put his sleeping bag in its sleeve and made a good-size freezer bag of jerky for him and Dawg. For water, he would eat snow for the night. It was no big deal; he had done that before.

He looked at Dawg out the kitchen window and wondered about the smell. Dawg would probably scare off anything that wanted to come in his direction. He also had the thought that the smell would attract more skunks. He smiled at the thought. Maybe he should take the Rocky along for help with the outlaws.

But the Kid had set his heart on sleeping under the stars waiting for the animal to reveal itself. He could not let Dawg and his smell stop him from all the fun of sleeping under the stars! He would make sure Dawg would sleep downwind and far enough away that the smell would be something he could deal with.

"June, have you got a copy, over?"

"Kid, you're early. What's up, over?"

"I finished my day and thought I would call early, over."

"How did your day go, and did you find any tracks, over?"

"My day went fine, and I did not find out anything on the tracks. That's why I am calling early. I am going to spend a few nights on top of the haystack and see if the animal shows up, over."

"Kid, it's still a little cold to be sleeping outside, over!"

"June, I like the cold. Well, now that it's not forty below zero, I still like it well enough, over."

"Kid, are you going to take the Winchester and that old canvas, over?"

"Yes, both and my lunatic Dawg with a skunklike fragrance, over."

"What did you end up using for the smell, over?"

"June, I found some condensed lime juice, over."

"Hey, that would work. You going take the Ugly with you and ride a horse back, over?"

"No, I thought I would walk to the stack. That is another reason I am calling early. I need to get going, over."

"You are going to walk with a good horse to get you there. It is your feet and be careful, over!"

"Thanks, if I take the Ugly, then Rocky will want to go. I just think it is better to take just Dawg, rather than the whole posse. I am in kind of a hurry, so I will talk to you tomorrow, over."

"OK, Kid, I will tell Paul what you are up to, and he will wish he was with you, I am sure, over."

The Kid put his sleeping bag and rolled-up canvas over his shoulder using the rawhide strap. In one hand he had Walker's Winchester and in the other the freezer bag of jerky. The Kid was prepared for all outcomes of spending the night under the stars.

As he walked through the ranch buildings, both Rocky and Ugly came, wanting to go along. The Kid rubbed behind both their ears and told them they would have to stay and watch the place for smelly outlaws. You just never know what gang would try to make the place their new hideout.

For the first time since he had arrived at the ranch, he closed the gates, going to where the bulls stayed. Walking a little way, he turned to see both his friends looking miserably at him and Dawg. He would not look back again—well, almost not look.

The Kid and Dawg walked the distance of about a mile in no time. They arrived at the haystack, which had already been set up to climb to the top. The Kid had used the tractor to clear some of the top layers off and made the top into a good, high, dry place for hiding and sleeping safely from what might be coming.

After fluffing up hay, the two adventurers made their individual soft beds and laid the canvas on top. The Kid laid the Winchester next to him and crawled into his sleeping bag. The canvas was another one of Walker's idea's. It was six by ten feet and waterproof. The canvas is laid on the ground, or in this case the hay, to keep the Kid separate from all the moisture from the ground and weather from Old Mother Nature. The Kid lay in the middle of the canvas with all his stuff, and if he wanted to, he could fold the canvas over him to shelter himself from all Mother Nature's wrath.

The Kid had needed something to keep him dry from the weather while watching over the sheep. Sheep, as the Kid found out, need a person to watch over them on most nights. The critters were always finding something to scare themselves into a wild frenzy over—most weather or the distant howl of a coyote. The Kid even resorted to playing the harmonica to help make the sheep fall asleep.

Walker had used the canvas himself a time or two and thought it would work for the Kid. The old cowboy even laughed, thinking the Kid would look like a hot dog lying in a bun with his head and feet sticking out from the edges. The Kid laughed and said he could curl up his legs.

There was still some sunlight left from the day, and the Kid got one of his books out from his pocket. Smiling, he shook the oats from between the pages. He was excited about being out under the stars waiting for the mystery animal to show up. He looked at Dawg wearing his pantyhose moccasins and told his friend, "The real outlaw is the cook in all the crazy pranks she has pulled on us!" A person could add up all the not-so-smart things he and Dawg had done. They would not come close to the stuff she had done and probably would continued to do if the Kid wasn't at the Hairpin. The pantyhose caper was just another in a long list of pranks that she has tried to get him to do. The Kid looked at Dawg, and he turned his head from side to side like always, trying to somehow understand what after all this time his Kid was trying to tell him.

There he was, looking at the millions of stars with Dawg eating jerky and thinking how he was so lucky to be where he was. He and his friends had for the most part made it through the worst part of the winter, at least the really cold temperatures. Now he was on top of a haystack hiding out. He might just get the chance to see what mystery animal was making the tracks.

He tried to theorize what wild animal could be making the tracks. It could be anything, maybe a rogue moose or elk. The hay he had pitched off the sleigh was gone, so whatever animal it was ate hay.

Then there were the original tracks that had started the whole mystery. The Kid knew that if Walker was able to see them, he would somehow have the experience to deduce what animal had made them, but he was not Walker. That was fine. It gave the Kid the excuse he needed to camp and break up a little bit of the winter routine. The Kid was finding out what Walker probably had liked about the ranch life during all his years. It was all the camping out. The cows or the sheep were the excuse he needed to be out in the open country sleeping under the stars.

Old Mother Nature's skies don't take long to make their change from daylight to dark. The Kid always liked pausing in all the day's activities to watch this process take place. The sun started to go down behind the snow-capped mountains first. Then as it went down, it seemed to fight the process and made its last-ditch effort to keep its colors visible in a glow of different colors. Now it was just a small amount of time till stars started to show up in ones and twos, with the moon getting brighter all the time. Then it was not long till the night sky was full of millions and millions of stars twinkling that seem to be there just for the viewing.

After rolling up into his canvas and snapping the edges together with Dawg looking at him, the Kid let out a deep breath of acceptance and said, "Come on." Dawg started at the bottom opening of the canvas and crawled, stepping on the Kid numerous times. There the two were with their heads next to each other. *Boy do you stink,* was the thought that came to the Kid's mind. They both waited under the moonlit night counting stars, hoping for any sound that might come to give away the approach of the mysterious owner of the tracks. They both fell asleep under the spell of the looking at the big dipper, dreaming of all things wild.

The Kid woke to the sound of coyotes barking. Dawg had already climbed from the canvas, growling at the noise. Grabbing the Winchester and slowly climbing out of his sleeping bag to have a look and listen, he patted Dawg a little to assure him everything was all right. The two listened as the coyotes communicated to each other from their different locations.

After a while, the Kid climbed back into his sleeping bag under the canvas. He had no idea what time of the night it was and thought he would try to listen to the night sounds as long as he could. This time Dawg laid on the outside of the canvas with his head on the Kid's chest as the coyotes barked their locations to each other. Dawg would communicate to the Kid his own dissatisfaction by showing his teeth and in a soft growl. The Kid smiled at his smelly friend having thoughts of protecting him from all the coyotes. He just talked low in a reassuring tone, saying, "It is fine. The coyotes are just saying how awful you smell. They can smell you all the way over there and cannot believe I am letting you sleep next to me." It wasn't long till the Kid was asleep with Dawg keeping a close watch for danger that maybe was close at hand.

Then, thinking it had only been a short amount of time, he suddenly woke to what sounded like animals walking close by the haystack. His instinct was to grab the Winchester and slowly climb out of from under the canvas, but where was Dawg? He laid on his back, trying to figure out the location of Dawg, all the while listening to the sounds. He was under the canvas where there was absolutely no light from the moon or anything else. The only thing he could think to do was start slowly coming out from under the canvas. He grabbed the Winchester and peeked out the top of the canvas to find it was daylight. He had overslept! After crawling to the edge of the haystack. He found Dawg and the rest of his posse of friends.

Shaking his head, he smiled at the scene of the grays and Ugly trying to get into the stack yard somehow. Dawg was still on top of the stack, as if saying, "Come on up, the view is great!" The Kid rolled up all his bedding and climbed down, with Dawg already saying his good mornings to his friends. There is just one question he had. How in the world did they make it through the gate? He hung his bedroll over his shoulder and started the walk home, with all his party crashers behind him.

It was not long till Rocky started checking the Kid's pockets for oats. The Kid had overslept, and Rocky needed his morning oat ration to get his morning started in the right direction. The Kid turned all his pockets inside out and let Rocky check all of his pockets somehow to stop all the grabbing at his clothes. Finally, the Kid smiled at Rocky and offered him some jerky. Walker had always tried worming Dawg with chew. Maybe jerky would work on the Rocky. Rocky just turned up his lips and smiled. The Kid laughed and climbed up on the Rock's back, and the race back to the ranch was on. All the friends ran the mile and through the open gate to the ranch.

He fed all the horses their oats and hung his bedding in the bunkhouse to dry for the next night's camp under the stars. The horses had somehow opened the gate and made it to the stack yard. He would tie it shut tonight with a piece of rope. Sleeping under the stars had the Kid relaxed and ready for the day's work. All he had to do was fix some breakfast and think of more excuses to sleep under the stars. He had a great old time!

After a few days passed, in preparation of camping out again atop the haystack, the tracker's work day went well and too slow, as is always the case when a person needs to be doing something besides work. The call to the cook had not taken long, and then he was out of the cookhouse walking to the stack yard. The only bit of information he needed to consider was the chance of snow from the cook's weather report. He thought that maybe the chance of snow might put off the night's camping. He just shook it off and said to himself that he had slept in worse weather herding sheep.

There were times he had slept under his canvas in complete downpours of rain and had stayed dry and warm. A person just had to dig a trench around the canvas and sleep with his or her head top to bottom downhill. The half-foot trench would give the rainwater a place to go and keep it off the canvas. The slope of the hill would help it run in the direction away from the canvas.

In the Kid's mind, water is water no matter if rain or snow. The one benefit of colder weather is no mosquitoes; he hated those little buzzing insects!

The little bugs were relentless in their pursuit of driving the Kid to the brink of madness. The Kid had been riding Ugly, a white horse, where the old war pony was just covered with blood from all the mosquitoes. The grays even had a set of leather fly netting they wore just for the express purpose of preventing the little bloodsuckers from biting them. The netting was made from thin strips of leather connected together that hung from the backs of the horses. When the horses moved, the netting would slide back and forth, killing flies or mosquitoes in its path, leaving a trail of blood. At the end of the day, the Kid would rinse the blood off the horses with water and brush them down like he had done for old Buttercup. He just thought it was a nice way of thanking the horses for the tough day fighting the bugs.

As far as bug sprays, there were a few different types of storebought remedies for mosquitoes, and the Kid had tried them all. He found the one he had come up with worked as well as any he had found. The Kid caught a clue from Walker on how to keep the mosquitoes away. Walker ate lots of hot, spicy food. One of Walker's favorite sandwiches was made from hot onions, mayo, and two slices of bread. The Kid just laughed. Walker said the Kid would come around to his way of thinking and start to like spicy food. Walker had the belief that all the spicy food he ate somehow made its way to his sweat; the bugs could not handle the combination.

Not being able to handle the hot food, he made his own concoction. He would soak hot onions in water and let all the juices mix together with the water. He would then fill a bottle with the witche's brew and then spray his clothes with the contents and the horses all over as well. He filled the spray bottle every morning and packed it with him for when the horses needed more, and it seemed to help. Walker told him that his concoction should help him out with the blond swimmer if he was ever to make it back to civilization.

So now snow might be coming. The Kid had survived all the wet weather herding sheep and oh my God, clouds of mosquitoes trailing cows. A little snow was not going to keep a cowboy from the chance of sleeping under old Mother Nature's starry night! Since the flatlander had arrived on the ranch, the weather had never stopped anybody from doing their job. The weather was just something a cowboy had to prepare for the best he can and then let the chips fall where they may.

The pair of friends was lying on their beds high atop the haystack, watching Old Mother Nature's evening skies start to cloud over. The Kid replayed his day of preparation for catching a glimpse of the mystery animal. First he tied one of his pigging ropes around the gate to keep it closed. The posse of friends was going to stay out of the stack yard tonight!

The next thing the Kid thought would help was to extend the trail of hay he had been leaving from the base of the foothills to stack yard. He pitched the small amount of hay closer and closer each day to the stack. Each day the hay was gone, and the bulls were not the ones doing the eating. Pretty soon the mystery animal would catch the clue to come and eat at the stack. Then the Kid would maybe catch sight of the animal or at least see a track he could make out.

The Kid watched as the clouds took over the night sky. The Kid was glad to have the little bit of light the snow gave off. Without the moon or clear skies, it was almost completely dark. He had not even considered taking a flashlight. As he thought about it, he had never seen any type of flashlight around the place to use anyway. Soon the snow started to fall, and the Kid wrapped up in his canvas with his smelly Dawg.

There is where the Kid and Dawg spent the rest of their night out under the stars, or it should be said the snow! Old Mother Nature's wind picked up, the temperature dropped a few degrees, and the Kid spent his night in one of the Big Hole bad winter storms!

He hunkered down under his canvas inside his sleeping bag, laughing at what Old Mother Nature was doing. The Kid lay on his back listening to the wind blow the snow horizontal over the haystack. He was glad he had made a deep depression in the hay to put his bedding. It was almost like listening to the station on the radio in all its sound effects; you just had to use your imagination a little to put yourself in the situation. The Kid laughed at himself at having the thought, because he was here and it's real!

There was no way any animal would be out in this weather. The jerky came out, and he shared some with Dawg. After a while, the Kid turned on his side with his back to Dawg. Dawg curled up next to the Kid's back, and that is how they slept the night through.

The next morning when he woke, all was dark under the canvas, and he listened to the morning sounds. He needed to get up and check the result of last night's storm but hesitated. He liked being all warm and dry under his canvas. The time was at hand for him to break the barrier of snow and come out from his night of hibernation. He unsnapped the top of his canvas and brushed the little bit of snow away. Dawg crawled his way out, followed by the Kid. They both looked over the result of the winter storm and smiled at how they had been so comfortable under the canvas.

The Kid looked around at the result of the storm. He saw only a couple inches more of snow and a little drifting. It was not bad for how the storm had started. He smiled, thinking it was maybe just the neighbors' snow again. The bulls were starting to come out from the willows where they spent the night together.

Then he noticed tracks that came from the direction of the foothills; it was here! It had walked all the way to the stack yard, eating the hay the Kid left on the trail back. The Kid quickly rolled up his bedding and slid off the stack. The tracks were fresh and made by a good-sized horse! The tracks were almost as big as the grays and roans would leave. He looked in the direction of the ranch, and there were no tracks that came from that direction. The mob had stayed at the ranch. These tracks came only from the direction of the foothills and not from any of his horses! The Kid's mystery animal was a horse. Could it be the old cowboy's wild black stud?

On the Kid's walk back to the ranch, he wondered how in the world a horse could survive in the mountains all winter. Then he wondered what circumstances caused the horse to be left there without being gathered up from summer pasture with the rest of the stock. He just shook his head at the thought of a ranch horse all winter in the mountains. There was not a chance. It had to be Paul's stud.

The Kid looked at the posse of horses waiting for him at the gate. He smiled at his friends and thought to himself, *How lucky you are to have a place to call home!* He opened the gate to the horses busting through the opening and running toward the haystack, with, of course, the Kid starting to the direction to the ranch.

It was Lucky who figured out the error in their plan. They stopped with heads turned and saw the Kid running to the ranch. There was now a race at which horse could get to the Kid faster and get his prize, oats. The Kid had to shut the barn door to keep the mob from running him over trying to get in. He slid the barn door closed just enough to see the only time in his life the horse had ever been first at anything—Rocky!

He filled the feed boxes with oats and one by one let the horses into the barn to their stalls. He laughed at the Rocky for winning the race and for the first time showing maybe he had more energy than he has let on.

Change Is A-Coming

After the long, hard winter, Old Mother Nature's humanity let spring arrive in the Big Hole Valley. She had finally given access to what the Kid felt was the most beautiful place he had ever been, with all its green meadows surrounded by snow-covered mountains.

The Kid discovered the Hairpin had three creeks, Fox Creek, Governor Creek, and Anders Creek. They all eventually ran to the Big Hole River. It was going to be great fishing.

Animals were starting to show up more and more each day— deer, moose, bear, and elk. The Kid thought the herd of elk was from over the mountain at the first summer pasture where he lost the old Dodge. He would ask Walker when he got the first chance to see if his guess was correct.

While riding old Ugly and checking the perimeter fence for breaks, he found the first of four cabins Walker had told him about. Everything the Kid needed—wood-burning cook stove, table and chairs, cupboards, and twin bed—was in relativity good shape. He thought the cabin would make a good cow camp for him to use.

The next old cabin, one that natives had given the name of the honeymoon cabin, needed more repairs than the Kid had time to mess with and looked somewhat newer even in its poor condition. The name made the Kid laugh at the thought of someone spending their honeymoon all the way up in the mountains. *Good idea,* was his thought on the matter.

The next cabin he found was just the bones of what the Kid thought had to be from an old homestead. As he walked through the rotted log walls, he tried to imagine the folks building the cabin. He tried to imagine why they had chosen this particular spot for their home and all they went through to get there to build the cabin.

The final cabin was all the way at the upper reaches of the ranch. Called the what, the fishing cabin, oh yeah. Cookie was in trouble now. It even looked like it had been used sometime in recent years. It was another place the Kid would camp and fish.

While starting to get know paradise, he remembered what Walker had mentioned to him a while back, that this would be a good place for him to work, the Hairpin. The Kid smiled at the memory and now realized how the old cowboy must have felt about his cow camp.

The flatlander Kid had spent many nights sitting on the ground cross-legged around his campfire listening to stories of his time spent cowboying. This place they call the Hairpin could turn out to be the Kid's place of adventure, hopefully give him his place to tell stories around a campfire.

When Old Mother Nature's spring finally arrived, he worked steady, preparing the Hairpin for the cow and calf pairs. Fences were repaired, irrigation ditches and head gates cleaned out, and pastures brushed using the grays; everything was ready.

Now he was most anxious. The time had come for the Kid to make his first pilgrimage back to the main ranch. It had been almost five months since he made his first trip into the Big Hole Valley.

He started his trip back to the main cookhouse for one of the cook's breakfasts before going on another cattle drive with the old cowboy. The two friends had only seen each other the one time when Walker brought his horses to him. It was far too long as far as the Kid was concerned.

The Kid sat talking to the cook about all his adventures, waiting for the door to open. He heard the dogs first, Sam and Helper. Then the old cowboy came through the back door looking the same as always: cowboy hat, silk bandana, heavy Levi jacket, and chaps, with the ever-present chewing tobacco stain in his gray-and-black beard.

Helper went between the Kid's legs to lie on her blanket under her new chair. All eyes were on the territorial dispute, and then Helper made her move.

She got him to say to her, "Hello, you're back." The Kid laughed at how fast the Helper still was and how he was out of practice. Everyone laughed.

All the hired help sat up at the table, looking at bowls of biscuits and gravy. The warm, flaky, golden brown biscuits were of the buttermilk type. The gravy was made from fresh whole milk thickened with flour and stirred in a skillet of grease and chopped up sausage.

The Kid paused, looking at the FLN cook with a raised eyebrow and a wry smile. Brains? She smiled back at his pause in a way that gave no clue if she was up to her old shenanigans. The Kid shook his head at the thought and piled his plate high. After a few bites, the Kid thought he had been eating peanut butter and jelly sandwiches for far too long.

The calves had already been branded and the cows worked through the chute, getting all their shots, while the Kid fixed fence preparing for the cattle. All that work was just a teaser for the Kid to trail the pairs to the Hairpin with Walker and all the other cowboys.

Even after all the cattle drives the Kid had been on since the beginning, the excitement of the all the cowboys trailing the cows still made the Kid think of old days past. He loved all the old landmarks around the area, Bannack the state capital, the Lewis and Clark trail, the Big Hole Battleground, and the old cowboy, his good friend Walker. The old timer now seemed to be as much a landmark in the Kid's life as the hanging tree is to the first state capital.

Once the cattle were on their way to the Hairpin, the two cowboys had a long talk while working the drag. The Kid had not seen any people during the winter and had built up a lot of conversation that needed to be let out. The old cowboy was just the willing recipient and smiled while the Kid told of all he had gone through during his long winter at the Hairpin.

After talking for awhile, there were two subjects left the Kid needed to talk to the old cowboy about: the elk and the tracks.

"Kid it sounds to me like you had a real good time working in that cold Big Hole weather!"

"Paul, I have two things I need to know. There is a herd of elk at the Hairpin that I think are the same ones from what I now call the lost old Dodge summer pasture. Didn't you tell me back then that elk herd came over to the Hairpin in the spring?"

"Kid, I did say that, and without having been at my old cow camp in a while, it's hard to tell for sure. How many elk are in the herd?"

"I have tried to get a count on them, but best as I can tell, about a hundred."

"Kid, that would make sense, because it has been a couple years since I have been working in that part of the country. We have all been there fishing and such. It's just not the same as when you live and work in that part of the country. You see more, as you have probably found out yourself working at the Hairpin."

"You're right about that, Paul. There are so many critters to check out! I cannot think I could have ended up in a better place."

"You said two things. What's the second, the horse tracks?"

"Yeah, how did you guess?"

"Kid, I may not like talking on that squawk box, but I can still hear what you are talking to the cook about."

"Paul, I probably shouldn't have mentioned the horse tracks over the radio."

"Kid, it is just like this, that wild stud and I have not been around each other a few years now. Since all of us left the old man's ranch, I have not been in that part of the country to see him. The tracks you saw could be his. I can't know for sure without looking at them. But when you talked to the cook about the tracks over the radio, everybody who has a radio and that was in the cookhouse heard you."

"Paul, I would think people around here would like to know there is a wild stud living free like the old days."

"Kid, the one thing I know for sure is that you cannot predict what people are going to think or do."

Walker waited for the Kid to finish and had news of his own for the Kid; the banker was in the process of selling the ranch. The news made the Kid stop his horse and ask the cowboy what happened to make the banker want to sell the ranch. Walker said that there was always speculation from all concerned as to why the banker was selling, and the old cowboy kept it all to himself. The one thing he did say was the new owner is an insurance company looking for more commercial investments in the cattle business.

The two cowboys talked for quite a spell about what might happen when the insurance company finally took over the reins of the ranch and how it would affect them both. The new owners would surely have different ways of doing things, and he would have to listen to the old cowboy's advice, just take things one day at a time and let things happen. If the Kid did not like the way things changed, there were plenty of ranches that need hired hands to help with the cattle work, but not like the Hairpin.

The change in ownership took the Kid back to that same issue before he left the first ranch: trust the old cowboy.

The memory was of when he needed to put Ike the cat in the burlap sack and take her to cow camp. Walker had told him how he was able to capture the lioness animal in a burlap sack. Trust the old cowboy.

Shrugging off the advice, he thought the more direct method of capture would work better for him. He decided to wait for Ike to start cleaning herself after the cat had her milk as a distraction. Then reaching over, he just very nonchalantly picked up the wild-ass cat by the nape of her neck, trying to put her in the burlap sack. The Kid could still remember the look on Ike's face—rage!

The awfully mad cat just about shredded the Kid's hand and arm. He even tried to drop the cat into the burlap sack, just to have her hang onto his clothes, inflicting more pain and suffering for his bad behavior of touching her.

She kept hanging onto his arm, and he kept trying to shake the lunatic cat off inside the burlap bag. He at the time thought it reminded him of trying to shake off a piece of tape that doesn't want to shake off. Finally, when she thought he had learned his lesson, she quietly walked off like nothing had happened.

The result of the Kid's mauling are scars to this day he still wears as badges of stupidity. There were scratches in places where he could not believe the cat could get to, like behind both elbows.

He was humiliated from the cat mauling, and the worst part was yet to happen. He had to take the bucket of milk to the cookhouse and the FLN cook. When he walked in the mudroom carrying the milk bucket, the tradition of pausing before breaching the invisible demarcation line took over.

Looking through the mudroom door with slumped shoulders, the Kid saw the FLN cook pointing to his chair, his time-honored first-aid chair.

The awfully nice and understanding FLN cook had showed remarkable restraint in giving the Kid any well-deserved I told you so's. She just looked at him, pointing to the chair, asking, "How many times does this make it now?"

The cook then just laughed again at what the flatlander Kid had thought he could get away with and said the worst thing the Kid could have wanted to hear: "Trust the old cowboy."

It took the Kid a couple more tries to have Ike finally in the burlap sack. He had done what the old cowboy suggested. He put a saucer of milk in the opening of the burlap sack and hoped like heck he could get Ike in from there. It took two tries.

So now he should just let the change in ownership go at whatever pace a situation like this was going to take. He would trust the old cowboy.

The Midwest flatlander had come a long way since the burlap sack whooping, a few years. Over the short time he had been ranching, he somehow had connected to the animals more than the people. He remembered all the animals he had connected with, like the first flatlander-kicking milk cow, dear, sweet Buttercup, the first really old horse that taught him how to ride, Old Brown, and finally the crazy, lunatic cat that almost tore his arms off, Ike. The only animal he could claim as his from that time on the old man's ranch was Dawg. But it was no different now than it was then. It was tough on the Kid to walk away from all his animals, and it could happen all over again.

The days had gone by quickly after the cattle were trailed to the Hairpin, with the Midwest flatlander Kid being all lined out for his summer. The new owners would have their staff in place once the ink was dry. He is to stay at the Hairpin doing the irrigating and fencing. The bona-fide cowboys from the main ranch would make trips over to look after the pairs, and if needed, he could come along to help out with the riding.

The first real change to the Kid's life was what he is doing now: waiting. It seemed the roans were going to be left at the Hairpin till the owners came to pick them up in the spring. They were the trash out- the-back-door people. The Kid had not put a lot of work into the horses and really had not had the time to make the friendships with them he had with the rest of the horses, so the investment in time and energy was no tangible loss.

But as the truck and trailer pulled away from the corral with the roans, the scene was most revealing as to things coming to pass for the Kid. With the new owner, what were the changes, and did they affect the Kid, his friends the grays, and the old war pony Ugly? The Kid had a real tough winter, and all his friends had made the time in paradise fly by with all their good-natured personalities.

He needed to get back to his day of work. That had not changed; there was always plenty of work on the ranch to make the time pass quickly. His day included fencing and spreading water over the fields.

But as he worked, the Kid was still excited about the horse tracks despite all the political changes that could affect him. Now that winter was over and all the snow was gone on the flat, the Kid was trying to get a glimpse of the wild stud; the horse still had to be around somewhere.

Now that the roans were gone and the rest of the stock were where they were supposed to be, the Kid could start staying at what would become his first cow camp.

The old Dodge was loaded full with all the fencing supplies, orange plastic dams, cleaning supplies, and a cooler full of food for his first night at his cow camp. As his old Dodge truck bounced down the dirt road, the Kid noticed a cow moose that soon would be weaning her calf. He looked at Dawg, smiling at what had to be the start of a lot of good nights camping out. The old Dodge kept bouncing up the road till he finally arrived at the first cabin. He unlocked the cabin door, letting Dawg have at any would-be nesters, and sat on the tail gate eating jerky while Dawg had his fun.

As the Kid scanned the upper part of the ranch, he saw pairs spread out all over the foothills eating green grass. Calves were bobbing their heads getting milk and playing like they had no care in the world. The little shavers had been through a lot and deserved to have a good time. He smiled at the thought. After the winter he had just put in, maybe a little fun was in order for the flatlander. The Kid looked a

little higher over the pairs, and even though the snow had melted off the level, it still covered the peaks that surrounded the ranch. What a place!

It did not take Dawg long to have packrats running out of the old cow cabin and homeless. The Kid spent the rest of his morning mortaring the openings between the logs and cleaning up the place to be able to move in.

When all his belongings had been moved in, he moved a four legged wicker-bottom chair to the little front porch, leaning its back against the cabin. It had been a good morning, and he sat back eating a peanut butter and bacon sandwich with chips, and to wash it down, he still had a little milk left that the cook gave him.

The Kid sat leaning back in the chair, thinking of all the other hired hands who had done the same thing. He laughed out loud, wondering how many were flatlanders from the Midwest. Probably none. He felt he had been given a chance of a lifetime.

The next project was the fire pit for cooking and sleeping under the stars reading his books. After herding sheep, he found different ways of making fire pits using what he could find. In most cases other then bad weather, he preferred cooking in his Dutch oven and iron skillets he had accumulated over his time camping out. Since the Kid was spending a lot of time in the upper parts of the ranch for the summer, he took the time to make the fire pit more permanent for cooking and sleeping under the stars.

The Kid looked at his handiwork and said, "I believe we're done with all our chores, Dawg. Let's go catch some fish for supper."

The pair walked into the distance playing. Dawg grabbed at his pant cuffs, and the Kid tried in desperation to keep from being pulled head over tea kettle.

As they approached the creek, he was happy to find the water had cleared up from all the spring runoff. The crystal-clear water gave way to all the different colors of greens, browns, and yellows that painted the creek's rock bed. That meant he could see his spinner moving down the creek and maybe catch his first relative of the Hairpin fish family.

By the time the Kid made it back to his cow camp, the Big Hole Valley's sun was setting over the tops of the snow-covered mountains. It was just another Montana sky washed in beautiful colors.

The Kid sat on his chair fixing one of his favorite meals, fresh fish and veggies. The cook would be proud. With his Dawg, the Kid got out a new book the cook had bought for him, one that he could add to his collection.

That night the Kid and Dawg slept under the stars next to his cow campfire dreaming of wild horses—horses that knew of no fences, had seen very few people, and ran free in the mountains.

Since moving to his own cow camp with Dawg, making all things good in the Kid's life, he would always in his mind be that Midwest flatlander that was only going to be just spending the summer.

What had kept the Kid working on the ranches for the most part was the old cowboy and his friendship. Walker had taken more time with him in friendship and showed him more respect than almost anybody else in his life so far. The Kid thought on many occasions that he knew why all the animals Walker worked with were so comfortable with him. It was from that very first moment of introduction that they all knew they were his friends and family.

Now he was in a situation that gave him the place and time to test and to verify what he thought he knew. All the teachings the old cowboy passed on to him had worked so far.

The Kid had almost duplicated all the techniques of winning a stock animal over with respect and friendship. Walker said to the Kid, "How you do and show that kindness depends on the animal and its history. You just have to take your time to listen if what the animal is trying to say works for him or her. They have different histories and personalities.

Already the horses were running around free and coming to him when the need arose for a day of work. He smiled at the thought of Rocky checking all his pockets, just knowing the Kid somehow keeps oats there just for him. The two friends had left the old man's ranch and where Walker had got his start, the place where he had his cow camp.

It was the place where the Kid sat around the old cowboy's campfire listening to so many stories of his adventures. The Kid felt like he should try to see if the Hairpin could be his place to call special, his cow camp. All summer he had worked hard at all his responsibilities of fencing and irrigation, looking for the chance to see any sign of the wild stud horse. He was somewhat disappointed not to see anything that resembled evidence the stud ever existed. The only possible conclusion was that the horse was somewhere over the mountain, maybe at the old cowboy's camp.

Since he had not taken a day off throughout the summer, he made plans to ride old Ugly that direction and see what he could see in that part of the country. Walker said the Hairpin and the main ranch had at one time connected to each other using grazing rights from the forest service. The Kid would ride as far as he could till dusk, spend the night, and turn around the next morning, starting for home. He made sure all his responsibilities were taken care of, and the day came for the Kid to go on his overnight expedition.

The first night he slept at the fishing cabin. That at least gave him that amount of a head start. There was plenty of jerky, the Winchester, and water from springs to drink from on the way. He was riding the old war pony, Ugly, and Dawg had the lead. The sun was just starting to come over the ridges, and the mosquitoes were still nowhere to be seen. It was a good start so far, and the Kid could not imagine thinking of anything more exciting than to track a wild horse in the mountains. Now all he had to do was find the tracks.

Like always, the Kid would sift through old memories of stories Walker had told him by the camp fire. Some detail from the stories might help him to come up with a clue to how the old cowboy would find the wild horse. The game of who is smarter.

The Kid laughed at himself for even thinking he had a chance of winning that game. The horse had lived here his whole life like the old cowboy and knew all matter of things the Kid had not even came close to understanding, like surviving through the winter in the Big Hole. But the Kid did have that one under his belt—just one winter.

The two sayings that kept coming to the Kid's mind were that you had to be smarter than Dawg and trust the old cowboy. The Kid smiled at the old cowboy always telling him, "Trust the old cowboy." He had always done something his way and should have done it the way the old cowboy had said. The Kid always paid some price for being hard-headed.

He said you had to be smarter than Dawg and in this case a wild horse. The Kid asked the old cowboy what he meant. His reply was to the point: always be a step ahead, know their next move, and be there waiting.

A person had to understand his opponent's way of thinking and the environment in which he or she lives. That meant you had to put yourself in the horse's shoes and how he would think in where he has chosen to live. A person could get almost nowhere in the game without that information.

As the Kid rode Ugly and with Dawg out front making all the squirrels sound off, he tried to think like the horse. Where he would like to be? What he would like to eat and where? After giving Ugly his head, thinking maybe the horse would have some ideas, they followed game trails up gullies, over creeks, and through trees. There was evidence of deer and elk and even a porcupine in a tree that looked at them passing his way, but there was no sign of any wild horse.

Now he had started to make mental notes on everything he found, just like he had practiced back at his cow camp. There he had taken the time to cover that part of the ranch with a fine-tooth comb. He knew where all the game trails the animals used were, where all their food and water sources were, where they went to roll in the mud to help with the flies and mosquitoes, and where they slept.

The Kid counted all the elk and found his original guess of one hundred was close. There were 114 elk, including calves. He knew where all the berries were that the bears would systematically eat in one spot and the next day start over where they finished the previous day. The Kid watched and inventoried it all.

To his disappointment, all his efforts looking for signs on the upper part of the Hairpin were pointless in acquiring evidence that the wild horse was around. Even the tracks from winter were gone that said the wild horse had ever existed.

Since he had exhausted all possibilities in the verification that the horse could be somewhere around in paradise, he decided to look more in the direction the original tracks had come from. This was why he has taken the time to expand his area into the direction of the main ranch and the old cowboy's cow camp. The horse had to be somewhere around.

He decided to stop on top of a ridge and have a look around the countryside. His view was full of trees and more trees with scattered open, grassy knobs. He lifted the saddle up on old Ugly to let the air under a little and then tightened the cinches back up and rode till the sun started to go down over the mountains.

The expedition had covered a lot of territory in the single day of riding. They had followed many different tracks: deer, elk, and even what the Kid thought to be bear scat from all the seeds. It was as much of a duplication of the inventory of signs from the upper part of the Hairpin at cow camp. There was no real change.

After the long day, Ugly was hobbled in some good grass eating his much-deserved oats. Dawg was trying to get as much jerky from his best friend as he could. The Kid sat by his fire wondering how close to the main ranch and Walker's cow camp he was.

After riding pretty much the whole day, he wondered if he should try tomorrow to reach one or the other of them. He would tease Dawg a little more, have something to eat by his campfire, and think on it till tomorrow.

The next morning showed signs of bad weather coming in his direction. There was high humidity with the smell of rain in the air. That made going any further from the Hairpin out of the question. The slicker went on, and he rolled up his bedding for the start back.

There was really no way of knowing how far he had come. He only knew how long it was going to take to get back: a full day. He thought maybe he would try to go directly to the cookhouse and skip going to his cow camp. He decided to go back maybe about a mile off the direction he had come to see if on the way back he might just come across something of interest.

He stepped into the stirrup, and the old war pony humped up to let him know weather was on the way. The Kid started laughing, thinking, *Ugly we don't have time for this.* Dawg, of course, did his best to aggravate the situation by trying to bite at his friends hooves.

After the old war pony was done with his little weather announcement, the Kid asked if he had a good time and that there was no use going through all that bucking. There were plenty of signs that the bad weather was already on its way. The old war pony stuck his nose down to the Kid, lying prone on the ground. They both looked at each other nose to nose, as if saying that had not happened in a while and he blamed Dawg for the event.

The Kid grabbed the old war pony's mane and pulled himself up off the ground. Dawg, in his ever-present friendship to the Kid and old Ugly, sat turning his head from side to side while the Kid got back in the saddle.

It had not been but a couple hours, and Old Mother Nature finally started to show her displeasure at the Kid. She, of course, being the mother of all things had every right to make the Kid feel her annoyance. The wild stud horse was able to survive all she could throw at him over the years—winters of brutally cold temperatures with snow blowing, dry fall weather with flies and mosquitoes that made the strongest of people shake their heads at their size and abundance, springs with mud so deep that a person could dig all he wanted and reach China before he could be able to dig enough to get the truck out.

So who did this young Midwest flatlander think he was? She had every right to make his trip as intense as she could while he looked for that wild horse. He needed to pay the same price or maybe more that the horse paid for living in her domain.

She thought the Kid showed remarkable resilience in surviving his first winter in the Big Hole Valley, her favorite home. But now the Kid showed signs of cockiness in thinking he could find the wild stud horse without

Mother Nature testing and making it harder for him. The wild horse earned the right to live anywhere from all the times he spent surviving her onslaught. Lord knows she did her best to make his life tough.

She needed to teach this young Midwest flatlander a lesson. She would throw at the Kid her summer arsenal of wind, downpouring rain, and most of all, her favorite thunder and lightning just for sound effects and flashes of light on his ride back to the ranch and safety.

The Kid lowered his head and pulled his hat brim down over his eyes. The weather had taken a turn for the worse, and he mumbled to his friends, "We're in the shit now."

Dawg had already started walking ahead in the direction of home. The old war pony had his Kid on his back and his best friend leading the way. It was time for the old war pony to dig in and remember how tough he used to be, the toughest bucking horse from the rodeo. The only cowboy Kid the old war pony would ever let ride him was on his back, and he needed to get him home safe and sound.

The time passed by in very slow minute-by-minute increments till it almost seemed to stand still. The hours and hours of horizontal wind with pouring rain made the Kid think he could be fortunate, that this could be snow. Then after that thought, he laughed because Old Mother Nature gave him a little thunder and lightning to light up her dark skies. The lightning displays were so outrageous the Kid had to stop and watch at what Old Mother Nature can do to make his day exciting. He counted the seconds between lightning and thunder one and two seconds pass by. Then there was a huge bang, making the ground shake and the Kid just a little nervous.

The hours passed by, with the Kid all hunched up in his slicker, letting his friends lead the way. Dawg was leading the way chasing squirrels and anything else that might strike his fancy, oblivious to the weather.

The Kid finally had to impose discipline and yelled, "You're the leader, you lunatic Dawg. Quit chasing the chatterboxes. Ugly, look at your best friend up there. He is supposed to be leading this expedition home, but he's chasing squirrels in all this weather." The old war pony just kept following his best friend, trying to go in the direction of home. The Kid in the end had to separate the two and ride Ugly back to where he thought the trail to the cookhouse was.

Dawg, Ugly, and the Kid's expedition had been in the timber, trying to make their way, with Old Mother Nature using all her bad mode, making the middle of day like darkness of night. The expedition could be going in the right direction or lost chasing squirrels. There was no way to tell. There was not enough daylight to see much of anything till he could get out of the trees. He just knew time should be on his side now after what he thought was late afternoon.

As the long hours passed, he started to see familiar landmarks, and a sense of relief hit him. It shouldn't be long now! The ranch buildings finally came into view, and the sight told the expedition and their ordeal was just about over. Their day spent dealing with the wrath of Old Mother Nature's bad mood was just another struggle for them to survive, strengthening their bond of friendship. Old Mother Nature, in all her magnificence, had made the day as hard to deal with as the worst day of the past winter.

As they approached the buildings, a sense accomplishment set in on the Kid; they were home. Then the nickering of horses welcomed the three weather-worn adventurers the rest of the way home. The grays and now the little bay came galloping to greet their friends, saying their hellos.

They all walked together to the barn, and the Kid was finally able to get down off the old war pony to stretch. He patted Ugly on his neck and whispered a thank you in his ear. He opened the barn door, and one by one, all the horses found their respective stalls. The Kid gave a few oats to each one, starting with the old war pony.

After brushing Ugly and turning all the horses out for the evening, he looked at Dawg, who was already sleeping on top of some loose hay. He was curled up, with his nose covered up by his tail. The Kid smiled and slowly picked his wet, dirty, stinky friend up and carried him to the cookhouse, never waking him up from his well-deserved sleep chasing squirrels.

"June have you a copy, over?"

"Hey, Kid, there you are. I have been trying to get a hold of you, over."

"Well, we made it back, and I am telling you one thing, I could not be happier, over."

"Sounds like you ran into the same bad weather that we have had over here all day, over."

"June, I have never seen the wind blow rain that hard, and the thunder and lightning was unbelievable! It was like the Fourth of July, but a whole lot bigger, over."

"Kid, I am glad you made it back all right. But the reason I have been trying to call you, is the new GM wants to get together with you. He has some changes he wants to talk to you about, over."

"Well I saw this coming for a while. Should I come over there, over?"

"No, he needs you to show him around the Hairpin, and he will call you on the phone tomorrow at suppertime, over."

"June, then I had better turn the ringer back on," he said, smiling.

"You know we have party lines over here, and I got tired of all the ringing noise from people calling each other, over."

"Kid, I can see it was probably a good idea to get you away from Paul when you moved to the Hairpin, over."

"Cookie, how's that, over?"

"Kid, he still thinks the telly is a newfangled invention, and you think the phone makes too much noise. How do you expect people to talk to you with the ringer off, over?"

"Cookie, we are talking now," he said, laughing, "over."

"Kid, you and that old, worn-out cowboy are far too much trouble for just one cook to have to deal with! Just turn the ringer back on the phone so the new boss can talk to you, and I will try to have something ready for him to bring you to eat when he comes, over."

Good-Byes

After the Kid finally received the call he had been dreading, June said it wasn't going to be long now. The Kid should come to the hospital to say good-bye on the last time he would see Paul.

As he drove, all manner of things ran through his head. What would he say to the old cowboy who taught him so much? Walker had showed the Kid how to milk the old Buttercup milk cow and ride his first horse, Old Brown.

The Kid for sure needed to tell him how important he was over the years in his life, how he had counseled him in all areas of life without any judgments and always with humor. Trust the old cowboy. Smiling, he thought if there was ever a time he should have trusted the old cowboy, it was about the lunatic cat Ike! There were so many memories of really great times the two friends had shared together running through his mind as he drove.

But as life happens, times change, and that was what happened when the Kid had his meeting with the new GM at the Hairpin. Walker told him to take one day at a time, letting things all unfold. Walker said that if you wait long enough, all things will eventually reveal themselves to you. There was no use fretting over the details till they became clear. Let life take its course, and that was what the Kid had done.

The changes that were to take place in the Kid's life were disheartening, to say the least. When the banker sold his ranch to the new owner, an insurance company, changes would have to happen. The Kid had always felt comfortable with that fact, but the depth of changes in all things that mattered to the Kid's life in paradise were far more than he could have ever anticipated.

All the changes that had happened paralleled the same changes the old cowboy had gone through when the old man passed and the grandson took over the reins. It was just life; you just had to deal with it the best way you could.

The Kid had in his mind tried to imagine the changes that would affect him. But as long as he could stay at the Hairpin with his friends, he could deal with them all. That was where the train falls off the tracks.

In the ownership change of the ranch, the grays were the property of the banker, and he would take them away to eastern Montana in the next few months.

Originally the old war pony Ugly was given to the Kid as a concession not to have the horse canned. There was no talk of giving the horse to the Kid for keeps, no bill of sale. The Kid just wanted to keep the horse from being canned, see if he could try some of the old cowboy's methods of working with the horse. Ugly now belonged to the new owners.

After all the ownership and corporate changes, the Kid decided it was finally time to move on, maybe try another ranch. After checking around the Big Hole Valley, the Kid ended up finding a ranch that from the first homesteaders did things the old west style, driving draft horses.

He wanted to learn how to drive a four-up hitch of draft horses, like a stagecoach. In the move, he had even found a big red daft horse, Chip, that he knew from the time back at the main ranch. He thought maybe he could get another chance at finding paradise.

The native family had even made him one of their family. It still wasn't the same. The grays were gone, and the old war pony Ugly belonged now to the new owners of the Hairpin. The Kid lasted only the winter before he finally made the move back to the big city.

After leaving the Hairpin, the Kid had some regrets. The first and foremost regret was of not doing enough to keep the old war pony Ugly. The Kid wished he had somehow tried to convince the new owners to sell him the horse before he left, but didn't. He at the time thought with starting over in the city, where would he keep the horse? Ugly was better off in the mountains, not somewhere in a rented field, and besides who could ride him? No one.

The Kid felt comfortable the banker would take good care of the grays. That was one of many things the Kid liked about the banker: he loved his animals, and the gray horses would never want for anything.

But as time flew by, the Kid wished he had taken the time to keep track of Rocky and Lucky, maybe somehow to say hello and take them some rolled oats, but he didn't. Once he moved back to the big city and to its fast pace, his life had become too busy.

The last regret the Kid had was the need to tell the old cowboy. It had been troubling him from the first day it happened on the radio. He had been so excited that maybe the tracks were from the wild stud horse and had talked on the radio about it. The Kid was so sorry for revealing the wild horse's location over the radio.

After that radio conversation, the Kid wanted to try the entire list of lessons the old cowboy had taught him about the wild horse, the game of who is smarter. Riding the war pony Ugly, he had tried tracking the wild stud through the mountains on different occasions, yet was never able to catch a glimpse of stud.

He lost all his hope of trying to best the wild horse in the ownership changes. The new GM had said no more overnight trips; he was there just for work. The Kid was even told he could not fish or hunt on the property; that also would take time away from work. The Kid accepted the changes with a little regret of losing some of his fun living in paradise.

Everything went along just fine for a time, till one day he stopped to visit the cook after a trip to town for perishables. The Kid stopped to get his canned goods from the main cookhouse and visit his old fishing buddy. It had been awhile.

When he walked into the cookhouse, June had a look of sympathy and some news. She said he should go look out in the corral and see what the cowboys had wrangled with a bunch of mares from summer pasture. The Kid thought his old fishing buddy was acting a little bit off and did as she had asked.

As he walked, all the hired hands were looking through corral rails at something—a horse. When he stopped, even though he had never seen the wild stud before, it surely was him. The wild horse stood in the farthest corner of the corral, pawing at the ground with his head down, looking like he was in the enemy's camp. The wild stud had fiery red eyes that were only enhanced by his coal black coat with long black mane and tail.

The flatlander Kid was as close to the wild horse as he could ever have imagined getting. He looked on in total amazement at what he was getting the chance to see. He thought he had been given the chance of a lifetime to be looking at the wild stud horse. He stayed for the longest time just watching the wild stud's every move and finally left for the Hairpin with all his groceries.

On the way back to the Hairpin, the Kid could only think about what the old cowboy had told him. You could never understand or predict what people were going to do. He felt a pang of fear in his gut, wondering what he could do.

By the next morning, the Midwest flatlander had decided to drive back to the main ranch and turn the wild stud loose. The Midwest flatlander had no plan other than he would just open as many gates in the fences as he could to set the wild horse free. He got up early to drive back to the main ranch before breakfast and before anyone had a chance to do anything about the horse.

When he had arrived back, the horse was not anywhere to be found. The only thing that was even making any sound was someone operating a D-6 caterpillar. He had a real sense of relief. By the time, he had looked everywhere for the horse. The Kid thought maybe Walker had the same idea as he did, to turn the horse loose as it should be. The wild horse just was gone, good for him!

The Kid watched as the main ranch came alive, deciding since he was there, maybe he would have one of the cook's breakfasts before he made the trip back.

Upon entering the cookhouse, June looked a little shocked at seeing him. He was supposed to be at the Hairpin, and what he was doing back? The Kid replied that he came back to do what Paul had done, turn the wild stud horse free. June showed genuine sorrow on her face at what the flatlander Kid said and had come all the way back to the main ranch to do. He asked June what she looked so sorrowful about. Her reply to the Kid still to this day hunts him.

After eating their supper, all the cowboys got together and tried to rope the wild horse, a rodeo. Through that process of ill advised male bravado, the cowboys had broken one of his legs. After watching the horse struggle for awhile with a broken leg, a hired hand finally had to shoot the wild stud horse, putting him out of his misery.

Everything in the cook's conversation beyond broken leg and shot was at the time very surreal for the Kid. He could not believe what the cook was telling him and questioned that maybe she was having a little fun with him. Her reply was that one of the hired men was intending to dig a grave with the caterpillar and bury the horse early this morning, to go have a look. Then the Kid knew it was true; he had heard the caterpillar working.

After the Kid realized it really had happened, without eating or saying good-bye, he left the main ranch, returning to the Hairpin.

After that day, the Kid finally realized the biggest change in the ranch being sold. The banker would never have let this happen, and the insurance company, for all its good intentions on making the change comfortable for everyone, probably had no clue that the incident had ever happened. After that day, the Kid and the old cowboy never brought up the wild horse in conversation again. It was now time for the Kid to say he is sorry.

As the Kid walked down the hall of the hospital, he saw June and some of her relatives hovering outside the old cowboy's door. When he approached his old fishing buddy, they hugged each other for a time.

"Kid, Paul will be glad you made it; he has not seen enough of you since you moved back to the city."

"June, I feel the same. I wish we could all go back to the way things used to be."

"Well you better get in there and don't give the old, worn-out cowboy any chewing tobacco. The old shit has been trying to get everybody who comes to visit to give him a chaw."

Almost smiling, the Kid opened the door to the old cowboy's hospital room to find the old cowboy asleep. Sitting down in one of the chairs, he looked at his old friend lying in the hospital bed. Feeling his heartstrings tugging, he bowed his head in his hands, looking away.

"Kid, where did all the women go?"

"Paul, they went to the café next door to eat and have a smoke. It looked like you were asleep."

"Yeah, Kid, I have been playing possum so the women would leave me alone. Now that you are here, get me my goddamn chewing tobacco!"

"Paul, you better quit talking like that! Besides, June said not to give you any, that I should ignore you."

"Kid, the women are outside smoking, and I am on my death bed, from what they all tell me! So after all these years of chewing the stuff, June now says the chewing tobacco could kill me while she smokes outside. Now do as I have asked and get my tobacco pouch!"

Shaking his head and smiling, the Kid did as instructed and got the old cowboy his tobacco pouch. Walker grabbed what was almost all that was left in the pouch and stuffed the chaw in his mouth.

"You know, Paul, it has not been all that many years ago that you tried to kill me with that stuff. So maybe June has a point, maybe try not to take such a big pinch."

"The women have been telling me I have been going to meet my maker for a while now. I would bet the man upstairs really couldn't care less how I talk and that I chew tobacco. Besides, I'll bet you never got any worms after that day you tried a chaw. It was the best thing that could have happened to a Midwest flatlander Kid at the time. How about you take what is left and we can break out of this place?"

"No thanks, now you're really trying to get me into all kinds of trouble with June."

"Kid, speaking of women, how's that blond swimmer of yours?"

"Paul, Nan is doing just fine. She got engaged to this little fellow that she met at work, an ankle biter."

"That is a shame; I thought that you and she would get hitched."

"I guess spending all those years apart changed me, but as it goes, we are still great friends. After spending all that time around you, I guess I liked my freedom too much to make my choice to get serious. Besides, I landed a job selling computers at a retail company, and that pretty much took all of my time."

"Kid, you like computers and can work them?"

"Paul, as you know, I am not the sharpest knife in the drawer. I just find computers make sense to me in how they work. It is as much of a surprise to me as it is to any of my friends."

"Kid, do you make better money than ranch work?" Paul asked, smiling.

"Paul, the money is fine. I just miss working with all the animals, and I need to say something now."

"Kid, you look really serious, so get what it is off your chest."

"Paul, we have never talked about the wild stud after that day, and now a few years have passed by. I would like to tell you I am so sorry for the horse being killed. It was my fault for talking on the radio."

"Kid, is that what you have been thinking all these years? That stud really was the last wild horse that lived around this area, so in that regard you are right in feeling bad that it could not be left alone to live out its days in peace.

"Kid, when the ranch sold, a whole new crop of people moved in, showing little respect for what was here already. I feel some connection to the horse being killed also, so do not feel you have to carry all the guilt.

"Times are a-changing, and there probably isn't any land left that people have not wandered into. So it was just a matter of time before that horse was going to be discovered by other folks. I am just sorry the ranch hands could not resist trying to rope him.

Kid, now let me say an apology to you for the Ugly horse, as you named him."

"Paul that was entirely my fault too! I should have asked the banker for a bill of sale."

"Kid, all people concerned knew that horse was yours. That is another thing that I hate about the change of new people coming here to live. There was a time a man's word was good and you could shake his hand to sign the deal, no bill of sale needed. That was the way of the banker and why it had never occurred to him you needed a bill of sale.

"Kid, when the new owners needed to cut back on all the horses on the ranch, the horses they had no use for sold or got canned to save on hay. Your Ugly horse was just got caught up in that bunch that got canned. Both June and I had no idea of what was going on at the time. She was busy cooking for all the hired men, and my health had started to fail. I am so sorry that your old war pony got mixed in with the canned horses."

"Paul, thanks. I have had a lot of time to think about all the animals and have come to these conclusions.

"Now as far as old Ugly, I wish I had tried to take him with me, but I didn't. I have to live with that! But he lived for what, another four, maybe five years? For most of those years he had a pretty good life on the ranch with me. I just hope the old war pony took some skin on his way out. God that horse was tough.

"Now that leaves the grays with the banker out east, close to the Montana border. I feel comfortable in saying that the banker will take good care of the grays. I miss them all very much and wish somehow I could go back changing things, but I can't. I am just lucky to still have Dawg in all his troublemaking antics." "Has he adapted to the city?" "Yeah, he thinks the place is for him to roam and meet chicks. Paul, I have never seen an animal do some of the things he does."

"You know, Kid, a dog takes after his master, so there is your answer! Kid, if there is one thing, I would say to you at what the women feel is my time to meet my maker, it is this: From the first day of meeting you, you made me laugh at the things you did. In my life, I have never met a Kid who tried butting heads with a yearling and then survive.

"But you laughed at yourself because you were having a great old time. Even when I almost killed you in town with chewing tobacco, you and I laughed till we could laugh no more. So let me now say, you were then and are now the best entertainment I have ever had the pleasure of having as a friend," he said, laughing.

"Oh my God, again with the I am just entertainment to the natives! I have worried what I would say to you on this, your last day. How much you have meant to me, how much you taught me about life, how wonderful it was to sit around your cow camp listening to you tell stories.

"I have dreaded coming here seeing you in the hospital for what seems like forever. You know, the women have been saying you have been dying for a while now," he said, laughing. "Now you tell me I was just entertainment! Paul, now tell me something serious that matches this day, your last from what the woman say."

"Kid, let me tell you something to help you with the ladies. Never do anything they say, especially if they say you're dying. It helps to keep them on their toes and guessing. I know I probably should have told you that a while back, maybe you would be hitched to that blond swimmer," Paul said, laughing.

"Well, that little bit of information is late in coming," the Kid said, also laughing.

"Kid, I hear the womenfolk are back from their smoking, so our time together is probably getting short. Let me say this now. I have already given you my pocket knife that you always borrowed to clean all the fish the cook caught in those contests of yours.

"Now I like it if you would accept my Winchester as a token of our friendship to remember this old cowboy. The rifle has a lot of good memories that I would like you to keep track of."

"Paul, I don't know what to say, so yes I would love to have the Winchester to remember you and the time we spent together."

"Kid, here is something else I want you to do for me. The Winchester is at the house with Sam and Helper. I have not seen my dogs in a while, and I like it if you would give them some attention and brush them for me. The soft horse brush should be in back of my old truck, if you would?"

"Paul, I would like to do that. But as you know I have never even petted Sam or Helper in all these years. After being gone, are they going to remember me? You know Sam will bite if aggravated."

"Kid, just let the dogs approach you first. Anyway, June has probably made them stay outside since I have been in the hospital. That will make it easier. They will remember your Dodge, and you have Dawg with you?"

"Yes, Dawg is in the truck."

"Then it is settled. Now there is one last favor I need of you. June and I have decided to spread our ashes at a spring that we are fond of in the mountains. The womenfolk tell me I am first to go," he said, smiling.

"There is going to be a lot of fuss, and that is not what we are about. I'd like it if you did not come.

"Kid, whatever you decide, please understand by not showing, you are probably going to get some flak from the natives. But Kid, I hope you agree, this should be our choice, how we should part company."

"Paul, I really would like to think of you as alive and riding your stud horse, trailing cows with Sam and Helper. If I would go to your memorial, I would lose that, and then my adventure with you would be over! Once you both are gone, then I will come visit and sit for a while, catching you two up on what is going on in my life."

After all the conversation, the Midwest flatlander cowboy Kid sat by the old cowboy's bed till he fell asleep from all the good company. He walked out of the hospital room to find June waiting with a little smile of sadness. They talked briefly, and the Kid left to keep his word to the old cowboy.

The Kid drove his old Dodge with automatic transmission, turning the last page of the story he had started all those years past. In it, the story had all the makings of something he should tell around a campfire in the mountains, maybe even to a kid not unlike himself, a Midwest flatlander. But time had to pass in order for life's grief to somehow let his heart mend, maybe a long time. As he approached, he saw Sam and Helper sitting on the tailgate of the old cowboy's truck, waiting for him to come home. Sam and Helper's old friend had never been gone this long, and surely he would have taken them along.

The dogs recognized the old cowboy's friend, and just like the first day he had met Sam and Helper, they started biting at his pant legs, saying hello. He smiled as if a huge weight lifted from his shoulders. He needed to feel something at that moment, and humor had always been his way.

He knelt down to give them both their first pat on the head in the time he had known them. After all this time that had passed between the old cowboy and the Kid, he had remembered what the old cowboy had asked of him on his first day: do not play with his animals. From that day on, the Kid had never wanted to get between the old cowboy and his animals; respect is what the Kid had been taught.

There they all sat on the tailgate of the old cowboy's truck. The Midwest flatlander cowboy Kid was still a little apprehensive. He first gave Sam and then Helper their much-awaited pats on the heads and scratches behind their ears. It had been a long-awaited brushing, and all parties were enjoying the quality time spent getting to know each for the first time.

Now it was time to get the old Winchester from the time he had spent with the old cowboy. He went to the door, looking to the dogs. "June says to leave you two outside, and by now she has figured out I gave Paul his chewing tobacco, so I am already in trouble with the cook." He let Sam and Helper in through the open door.

The Kid walked into the house and found the old Winchester leaning next to the old cowboy's leather reclining chair as if that was where he was supposed to find it. He just stood looking at the old rifle, knowing if he picked it up that was it; his adventure was all over. Slowly shaking his head, he picked up the rifle and sat in the old cowboy's recliner.

The moment was as sentimental as he could ever have imagined. There he was sitting holding the old cowboy's Winchester with his dogs, Sam and Helper, by the recliner on their horse blankets. He closed his eyes to make the moment somehow easier to take in. This was the last, and there were no more.

After a short time, he opened his eyes to find Sam and Helper sitting in front of him, as if asking for something. "Well, you are already in the house. You might as well sit in Paul's recliner with me." The dogs jumped to each side of the Kid, sitting in the recliner.

"You know, you two are going to get me in all kinds of trouble with cook! I am afraid this little escapade could be your last time in the house, and if we get caught probably mine too, so let's enjoy." That is where they slept, the Kid holding the old Winchester with the old cowboy's dogs by his side.

The end

Thank You Credits

Mom and Pops	adopted parents
Dick	best friend
Dick's relatives	draw card
Nan Hawthorne	best friend
June and Paul Walker	FLN best friends
Sam and Helper	FLN best friends' dogs
Dawg	first best Dawg
Louis L'Amour books	all kinds of childhood heroes
John Wayne characters	childhood heroes
Clint Eastwood characters	childhood heroes
Dick Butkus	childhood hero
Rocky Balboa	childhood hero
Old Buttercup the milk cow	first Kid-kicking milk cow
Old Brown	first cow horse
Ike the wild-ass cat	first lunatic cat
Ugly	first rodeo bucking horse
Rocky and Lucky	first draft horse team
Sunny and Red	second draft horse team
Little Bay	innocent bystander
Head-butter yearling	entertainment
Butchered steer Butkus	sacrificed internal organs
Wild deer	jerky
Fish	never caught enough to win
Geologists	misplaced old Dodge truck
Outlaw skunks	smelly entertainment
Banker	a riot to work for
Wild stud horse	wish it had not happened

Printed by Libri Plureos GmbH in Hamburg, Germany